Anne Ross brings to life the clinical list of symptoms and problems of Asperger's: rigidity, perseveration, tactile defensiveness, clumsiness, concrete thinking, and more, with remarkable honesty that can be painful but also humorous. This is a book that every parent of a child on the spectrum can relate to and every professional who works with these kids can learn from.

—Mimi W. Lou, Ph.D., clinical psychologist and former director of Children's Hospital Autism Intervention, Oakland, California

Anne Ross writes with honesty and intimacy reminiscent of friendship, and without sentimentality she captures how humbling it is be a parent. A psychologist working with families, Ross shows fellow professionals that a dose of humility can increase our effectiveness tenfold, delivering this message through vivid storytelling more lasting and impressive than any lesson learned in graduate school. This book and the real people in it will stay with you long after you've turned the last page.

—Jennifer Simmons, M.S., BCBA, school psychologist; licensed educational psychologist; Board Certified School Neuropsychologist, Northern California Assessment Center for the Deaf

Valuable insight from a parent and psychologist in the trenches. I wish I had this book when my son was diagnosed with autism. Honest, riveting, and instructive. A must-read for new autism parents.

—Laura Shumaker, author of *A Regular Guy: Growing Up with Autism* and SFGate.com Autism and Disabilities Writer

Anne Ross captures perfectly what it feels like to be on both sides of the table—as a public school special education expert and as a parent of a child who required special education. Her story is both heartbreaking and joyful, and she generously shares it so that other families' passages through child raising will be made smoother.

—Rebecca Branstetter, Ph.D., educational and clinical psychologist and author of *The School Psychologist's Survival Guide*, *The Teachable Moment*, and *The Everything Parent's Guide to Children with Executive Functioning Disorder*

Beyond
Rain Man

———

For Mom,
Love "Anne"

Beyond

Rain Man

WHAT ONE PSYCHOLOGIST LEARNED
RAISING A SON ON
THE AUTISM SPECTRUM

———

ANNE K. ROSS

LEATHERBACK PRESS

EL CERRITO, CALIFORNIA

Anne K. Ross/Leatherback Press
El Cerrito, California
www.beyondrainman.com

Cover by 1106 Design
Interior by Stacey Aaronson

The author is not rendering professional advice or services to the individual reader. The ideas, procedures, and suggestions contained in this book are not intended as a substitute for consulting with your physician. All matters regarding your health require medical supervision. The author shall not be liable or responsible for any loss or damage allegedly arising from any information or suggestions in this book.

Names and identifying details have been changed to protect the privacy of individuals who appear in this memoir. The author is using a pen name to honor her son's wishes. This story is true.

Publisher's Cataloging-in-Publication data

Names: Ross, Anne K.
Title: Beyond Rain Man : what one psychologist learned raising a son on the Autism spectrum / by Anne K. Ross.
Description: El Cerrito [California] : Leatherback Press, 2016 | Includes bibliographical references.
Identifiers: ISBN 978-0-9970400-0-5.
Subjects: LCSH: Parents of autistic children—Biography. | Autism in children—Treatment. | Autism. | Autistic children—Family relationships. | Parenting. | Children with disabilities—Family relationships. | Parents of children with disabilities—Attitudes. | Child rearing—Psychological aspects. GSAFD: Autobiographical. | BISAC: BIOGRAPHY & AUTOBIOGRAPHY / Personal Memoirs | EDUCATION / Special Education / Developmental & Intellectual Disabilities | FAMILY & RELATIONSHIPS / Autism Spectrum Disorders | PSYCHOLOGY/ Assessment, Testing & Measurement.
Classification: LCC: RJ506.A9 .R67 2016 | DDC: 616.85/8820092—dc23

Beyond Rain Man/Anne K. Ross.—1st ed.

ISBN 978-0-9970400-0-5
ISBN 978-0-9970400-1-2 (ebook)

For all the families who are finding their way.

1

———

Inklings

A FEW YEARS AGO, AT ONE OF MY ELEMENTARY SCHOOLS, I met with the parents of a first grader to go over their son's test results. In the music room I used as an office at that school, the couple settled across from me at a low table, our knees barely fitting underneath. It was the table where I worked with children, giving them IQ tests and asking them to write and draw for me. It was the table where teams of us— teachers, the speech and language pathologist, the occupational therapist, the principal, and others—met to discuss children who needed extra attention at school. It was the table where I ate my lunch while scoring test protocols and answering emails.

The boy's father was a larger version of his son: a burly guy with short black hair and skin rosy from lots of outdoor activity, wearing khaki shorts and a polo shirt. The boy's mother was petite, carefully made up and dressed for work in a navy skirt set. I knew from the developmental history they had filled out that she was a lawyer and that he had left his contractor job to manage the kids and house. As I opened my file folder and arranged some test protocols in front of me, he bent a large leg over the other, leaned back in the small chair, and crossed his arms. When I glanced up, her hands were shaking.

Their son, at six, was a math whiz with perfectly average intelligence and above average attention to details—he loved Legos and knew a lot of facts about dinosaurs. He had a couple of friends from preschool with whom he loved to play chase on the playground.

I started with these strengths as I went over my test results with these parents, showing them charts so they could see how their boy was just like his classmates in many ways. "He worked very hard on the tests," I said. "And when we took a break, he told me jokes that made me laugh out loud."

Across the table from me, they both smiled, and the boy's father uncrossed his arms.

After thirty years as a school psychologist in the San Francisco Bay Area, I have now sat across a table from over a thousand schoolchildren. I started this gig at twenty-seven, wearing skirts or dress slacks and silky blouses, my thick blonde hair woven into a braid that hung to the middle of my back. I was ridiculously earnest, proud of being a grown-up, and petrified about whether I would be good at the career I'd just begun. I knew sign language from my work at a deaf school, and I tested deaf kids and hearing kids. I tested poor kids and rich kids. I tested kids with mental retardation and kids with IQs in the 120s and a few in the 130s. And once, a fifth grade boy with an IQ of 145. I have tested kids—and continue to test kids—in order to identify learning disabilities and emotional disturbances, and particularly in the last decade, to recognize autism spectrum disorders, the fastest-growing special education category of school-aged kids. I've worked at preschools, elementary schools, middle schools, and high schools. I've worked in the inner city and in affluent neighborhoods. My first year, 1984, I was assigned to seven schools, and I drove from school to school to school, test kits sliding around in the trunk of my bile-colored Datsun Honey Bee, mixed in with my hiking boots, 35 mm camera, and my dog's water bowl.

Meeting with the first grader's parents now, I moved my swivel chair back from the table and crossed my legs at the knees. No more skirts for me; I wore only slacks, sometimes even presentable jeans, and almost always my black clogs. My hair was shorter and so was my stamina for the mentally draining work of a school psychologist. But I hadn't lost the deep desire to do meaningful work.

"Ben processes some information slower than his peers," I said, showing them the numbers on the bell curve chart. "He also has trouble reading the other kids' facial expressions. You know about the meltdowns here when things don't go his way or when he makes a mistake." They nodded in unison. "He's sensitive when his classmates use loud voices, and he doesn't tolerate kids brushing up against him in line." They both locked eyes with me, waiting. "His teachers told me about his frustration with writing and with moving on to each new activity. He shouts or cries or pouts when asked to make changes. And when you describe his getting stuck on how things have to be at home, his desperate need for routines that he can count on, how when he was little he didn't look right at you and didn't follow what you were looking at, well, all these things lead me to believe he is on the autism spectrum."

I paused for a few seconds. No matter how many times I say this, it still makes my heart race each time. I'm not sure if a father will scowl and insist, "Not my son," or if a mother will cry and say that Doctor So-and-So said it wasn't autism, or if they will thank me for my thorough work and tell me they knew something was not right and that this now makes perfect sense.

"Has anyone ever mentioned this possibility to you?" I asked now.

Often at this question, parents tell me about doctors who have dismissed their reports of tantrums or toe walking or unusual love of spinning, or sensitivity to noises and clothing as perfectly normal developmental stages. Sometimes I hear about preschool teachers who suspected something was not quite right: a child insisting on certain routines, like needing to arrange the toy cars in a peculiar manner, all lined up in the same order, upon arrival each morning. Sometimes I hear about other family members—aunts or uncles or cousins—with similar quirky traits.

These parents shook their heads. "No," his father said, crossing his arms again. "This was not on our radar."

"It's sometimes tough to figure it out with kids who are at the high end of the spectrum," I explained and then launched into my talk about how broad the spectrum is and how many highly successful people—both in history and currently—are now thought to be on the autism spectrum. Maybe Einstein and Mozart. NASA folks. A good chunk of Silicon Valley. "People on the spectrum often do extremely well in life," I said.

"We waited, we didn't ask for the assessment until now," the boy's mother said, wiping away a tear that had threatened to spill over. "We thought it was a stage. Maybe we should have done something sooner."

"How could we have known?" the boy's father asked.

"I should have known," she said, placing a hand over her heart and patting gently. "I'm his mother. Mothers are supposed to know."

At some point in each of these parent interviews, there comes a time when I decide whether or not I will share my

story. Sometimes I don't share it at all. But sometimes I feel I
need to, for the authority it will bring me with skeptical
parents. And sometimes I do it in order to maintain rapport so
we can work together on how to help their child learn. But this
mother needed something else.

"I have a son—a teenager—who's on the autism spectrum."
They stared at me as if this was impossible, the professional
across from them having a son like theirs. "We got the diagnosis of Asperger's when he was eleven," I said, immediately
remembering the cold cement floor of the huge bookstore on
which I sat for two hours after we got the news, pulling books
off the shelf and skimming them fiercely, desperate to know if
it was true, if my kid had this thing I didn't even know how to
spell.

"I should have known what it was," I said to the couple.
"I'm a school psychologist. I should have known."

But back then we didn't know what we now know. When I
trained in the early eighties, autism meant kids twiddling their
fingers in front of their faces, making odd vocal sounds but no
words. In my master's program in the early eighties, we read
about the cold, withholding "refrigerator mother" causing
autism. The mother was always getting blamed back then, for
homosexuality, for schizophrenia, for autism.

"It gets better," I told the couple. "It definitely gets better.
He's in college now, having some trouble managing the work-
load, but things are so much better." My son Matt had just
texted me the week before: *I continue to live, learn, and change.*
And realizing this made me break into a genuine smile, one
that comes from feeling happy, not one that comes from trying
to make others happy. It was true. After the years of fists
through walls, a broken mirror and a broken toe, and calls to
the police, it had gotten better. But I didn't want to tell them

about those scary times or the ambulance. Their son would be different in most ways; no two people on the autism spectrum are exactly the same.

It was enough for the parents of the first grader that day. Before they left my room, the boy's mother came around the table and opened her arms for an embrace. She squeezed and then let go. "It makes me feel so much better that you know what we're going through."

"But he's on the really high end of the spectrum, right?" the boy's father asked. "I mean, we're not supposed to go home and freak out about this, are we? He's on the really high end of the spectrum. Isn't that what you said?"

"No, you don't need to freak out," I said. "You might feel a bunch of things. You might feel sad or confused or even upset at me for bringing you this news, but you also might feel relieved. Relieved to know what it is that's been causing his emotional outbursts, his getting 'stuck' on everything."

He shook my hand for a long time. "I just want to make sure I have this straight," he said, his eyes boring into mine. "He's on the really high end of the spectrum, right?"

As a young woman, I imagined my future self as a successful career woman and a perfect mother. I had not yet heard the term *good enough mother*, but if I had, I probably still would have aimed for perfect. Even now, I'm still trying to lose the fastidiousness, but it doesn't seem to be working; it's apparently deep-rooted, genetic probably. My family's gene pool tends toward the persnickety.

I never imagined that years later—after quitting college in Indiana and moving to San Francisco, volunteering with children with autism, earning a master's degree in educational psychology and then a doctorate in clinical psychology—I would be a career school psychologist who would call the police on her own teenaged son, follow an ambulance carrying him to a psychiatric hospital, plan to send him away, and cry so hard all the muscles in my face ached. I never imagined the times I would feel far from perfect, or the times I believed I had utterly failed.

On Saturdays in the late 1970s, when I was in my early twenties, I volunteered at the Recreation Center for the Handicapped in San Francisco helping out with a group of boys with autism. Jeremy mimicked television commercials. "Visine," he'd say, "gets the red out." Long-lashed, fair-haired Danny would only eat a tuna sandwich, cut in fourths, a phenobarbital tablet for his epilepsy hidden inside one of the tuna triangles. One boy was taller than me and hugged too hard. Another sank his teeth into the heel of his hand when upset; it had grown a thick callus. Alan, the only boy who talked to us adults, talked so much we sometimes had to ask him to be quiet. Some of them flapped their arms. Most repeated what I said with a special affinity for the last words in my sentence. (Me: "Hold my hand when we cross the street." Him: "Cross the street.")[1] We took the boys to the zoo, to the beach, to the mountains to play in the snow. I knew nothing then about special education, goals, performance measures, psychoeducational testing, or school psychologists. I wanted to be a teacher. I was idealistic, passionate, and naïve. My favorite book in college was Virginia Axline's *Dibs in Search of Self*, and I, too, wanted to cure children lost inside themselves.

---

[1] This is known as echolalia, or the immediate, or delayed, repetition of words spoken by another person.

Around that time, I stuck a bumper sticker on my Datsun Honey Bee that read: I'D RATHER BE STIMMING. I loved it for its abstruseness, for the private joke. Stimming is what children with autism do: hand-flapping, head-banging, humming, finger-twiddling, spinning toys, waving a piece of yarn in front of one's face. One day, I stopped at a red light on my way home from work at the California School for the Deaf, and a young man on a motorcycle pulled up next to me. Over the drone of his engine, he shouted, "What's stimming?" I wasn't sure how to answer in the time before the light changed. "Self-stimulation!" I shouted across the lane as the light turned green. He smiled hugely. "Well, all right!" he said, revving his engine and speeding away. "Wait!" I pleaded. "I didn't mean it that way!"

After the parents of the first grader left, I distributed my report to the rest of the team. We would meet the following week to develop a special education plan to help him manage his school day. These parents were now part of our team, and we'd work together on getting him the therapies he needed and making some accommodations for the way his brain worked a little differently. But it's not always like this. We're not always able to work with parents when they don't accept our findings, when they need to hold on to an earlier explanation, one that may not be the right one.

The year before, a clinical psychologist attended a school meeting for a fifth grade boy the team had evaluated. He wore a tailored suit, his graying hair slicked back with a smelly product. He'd come because the school's speech and language therapist and I had informed the boy's parents that we believed their son's insistence on routines, robotic tone of voice, overly formal greetings with peers—along with an interest in medieval warships so intense that his father characterized it as *an inch wide and a mile deep*—were better explained by the autism spectrum rather than the psychologist's diagnoses of OCD[2] and ADHD.[3] My test scores showed learning patterns consistent with a child with a smart, autistic brain. The speech and language pathologist tried to explain to the boy's parents how his lack of close friendships and poor pragmatics[4] were also strong indicators. He stood too close when talking with others, didn't use typical facial expressions, and didn't understand sarcasm or idioms.

"He's not autistic!" the psychologist said, smacking his palm on the table. "I've been treating children for twenty years. He has OCD and ADHD. I've known him since he was three years old."

We can only see what we know. He apparently had not kept up with the field of autism and how the specific behaviors show up in a variety of combinations and varying degrees of impairment in each person. He was stuck back in an earlier day when autism referred to more obvious behaviors, when it described children like the boys I had volunteered with in San Francisco. Sometimes I wonder what condition I might still miss because I don't know it like I know autism. School psychologists and clinical psychologists utilize different diagnostic categories and identify children for different purposes, but we're all familiar with the array of possibilities, like attention deficits, mood disorders, conduct disorder, depression, anxiety. We're familiar with some more than others, depending on our particular experiences working in schools or clinics, with preschoolers or high schoolers.

---

[2] Obsessive compulsive disorder.

[3] Attention deficit disorder hyperactivity.

[4] The social use of language.

"I noticed in his earlier reports that you gave him a PDD-NOS[5] diagnosis," I said, trying to find a diplomatic way to say what I really thought: *What the hell's wrong with you now and why did you waver?* Instead I said, "You mentioned his fascination with wheels and his echolalia."

"Oh, he was so young then. Now we have a better idea of what's going on."

Exactly! I thought. Autism spectrum disorders are present from birth, usually (but not always) observable by age three years. He didn't seem to understand that autism doesn't simply disappear; instead it often morphs into something less recognizable. As children develop, they typically show fewer quirky behaviors. They don't completely grow out of autism, but they often compensate for their difficulties with their strengths. And while they are growing up, many kids are trained formally by speech and language pathologists and occupational therapists, and many are trained informally by parents who don't even realize they are teaching their children when they insist on eye contact and when they model social greetings. By the time children get to the end of elementary school and enter middle school, their autism-related behaviors are sometimes difficult to spot.

"Yes," I said. "When we trained, autism was a much narrower diagnosis—"

"Some of my patients have come back very angry about being misdiagnosed with autism," he said. "One of them came into my office in tears and said, 'I'm not Rain Man.'" The psychologist stared hard at me. "This ridiculous 'Power to the Aspies' movement is harmful to my patients. This label is being overused," he said.

---

[5] Pervasive developmental disorder-not otherwise specified.

Rain Man? He was comparing our student, and his other patients, to an autistic savant character in a 1988 movie who could memorize pages of the phone book and count cards from a six-deck shoe in Las Vegas. Savants—not all have autism—are extremely rare.[6] Dustin Hoffman's *Rain Man* character doesn't come close to representing the wide range of individuals on the spectrum and how we now understand the heterogeneity of the population.

I was stunned. What could I possibly say in front of the boy's parents, parents who clung to their therapist's denial of a feared diagnosis? *You don't know what you're talking about?* I wanted to argue that more kids are being missed—undiagnosed or incorrectly diagnosed—than are being overdiagnosed with an autism spectrum disorder. That every school year I see a half dozen middle school and high school students who clearly fall somewhere on the spectrum but whose parents or physicians still hold onto a salad diagnosis: a handful of ADHD, a dash of obsessive compulsiveness, a sprinkling of pragmatics disorder, dressed with anxiety,[7] and with a side of stubbornness. These are highly educated, well-respected practitioners who don't yet know how to put it all together and accurately name it.

I wanted to tell these parents that the Asperger's label had only benefited my own family. It allowed us a better understanding of our kid and helped us find people who knew how to teach us. And it brought a sense of relief to Matt. He finally

---

[6] The phenomenon is found in about ten percent of people with autism and in less than one percent in those without autism, according to the Autism Research Institute.

[7] Anxiety is one of the most commonly co-occurring disabling conditions experienced by people with autism spectrum disorders. They show symptoms of specific phobias, obsessive compulsive disorder, agoraphobia, generalized anxiety disorder, and social anxiety disorder. Anxiety is thought to contribute to repetitive behaviors, insistence on routine, and explosive behaviors.

had a name for what was causing his social confusion and
emotional distress. And he finally had the knowledge that he
was not alone.

But it wasn't the right time or place for me to educate this
family. They were holding tight to what they needed to believe.
When the boy's father stood to leave the meeting after two-
and-a-half hours, he took the psychologist's hand in his as if
he were a brother. "He's like family," his wife explained. The
speech and language pathologist and I straightened our papers
and put our reports away. This one would take some time.

These kinds of meetings exhaust me. I lie awake at night
fretting about the families who are led astray, usually benignly,
sometimes for years, often from a professional's ignorance.[8]
Most of all, I'm frustrated by the loss of time for some children. Time when he or she could be getting the right therapies instead of being treated (and medicated) for something
they don't have. I soothe my bruised ego by telling myself that
perhaps eventually families like this one will put it all together
—maybe by middle school when the social demands for kids
ramp up and become more sophisticated, when peers can
become cruel, or maybe by high school when their teen still
doesn't know how to make friends. I hold out hope that they
have a more accurate picture of their child by the time he gets
to college so he can advocate for himself when he needs to tell
a professor how he learns best and what accommodations he
might need. Mostly, I want them to have the right information

---

[8] With tools like the M-CHAT-R/F (Modified Checklist for Autism in Toddlers,
Revised with Follow-Up), pediatricians and psychologists can screen for autism
in children as young as 16 months, when intervention can still change brain
structure. (Screenings like the M-CHAT-R/F may not be sensitive enough for
children on the higher end of the autism spectrum, however.)

so that their child can begin to understand himself[9] and how he wants to fit into the world.

In 1992, the year before my first son was born, the category of "autism" was added to the California Education Code as a distinct special education eligibility category; the list already included learning disabilities, speech or language impairments, mental retardation, deafness, blindness, and multiple disabilities.

According to the U.S. Department of Education, in 1992 there were approximately 5,000 school-age children classified with autism in the United States. I'd only seen one student with autism in my first eight years as a school psychologist. Or so I'd thought. As I look back now, though, I wonder how many I missed.

By 1993, the year Matt was born, the number of children in special education in the United States due to autism had tripled since the year before. It was about 15,000. By 2000, the number was 65,000, and in 2011 it was 417,000.[10]

When I started working as a school psychologist in 1984, autism was diagnosed in 1 of every 10,000 children in the United States, according to the CDC.[11] Twenty years later, by

---

[9] I use the male pronoun most often because of the higher diagnosis rate for males (4:1). The diagnosis rate difference is thought to be due to anatomical gender differences (see Simon Baron-Cohen's book *The Essential Difference*). Recent studies using brain imaging suggest that male brains are more vulnerable to autism triggers than female brains. (See, for example, "Why it's not 'Rain Woman'" in *The Economist*, March 1, 2014.) Also, since high-functioning girls on the spectrum present differently than boys on the spectrum, they may be underdiagnosed. Their social use of language, for example, often appears typical until it is closely examined. They also may present with fewer restricted interests, and those interests might be more typical of their gender and age (for example, pop stars, horses, make-up, clothing).

[10] U.S. Department of Education, National Center for Education Statistics (2012).

[11] Centers for Disease Control and Prevention.

the 2003–2004 school year, it was up to 1 in every 166. In 2007, 1 in 150 children were diagnosed with autism. Then, using data from 2008 released in 2012, it was 1 in 88. The estimate for boys at that time was 1 in 50. Three years later, in 2015, using data collected by the CDC in 2010, the incidence rate had climbed to 1 in 68 children, with 1 in 42 boys being identified as being on the autism spectrum. The rate had more than doubled over a decade.[12]

Occasionally, after my psychoeducational evaluation of a student, a teacher has doubted my conclusion that the boy or girl was on the spectrum. "She's so social," they might say. "He engages just fine with me, and his eye contact is good." I feel defensive at these moments, defensive of my work, my knowledge, my experience. I try to educate people about the breadth of the spectrum, the subtle signs that delineate the disorder, how it presents in boys and how it presents in girls. Every time the CDC releases higher autism incidence rates, though, I feel secretly vindicated. "See?" I want to shout. "One in 68! We haven't even identified all of them." But of course I don't. Instead, one student at a time, I meet with parents to give them information that I hope will help them take care of their kids.

Finally, after years of conjecture about what is causing the huge increase in number of kids on the spectrum, researchers are documenting what I'd suspected for some time: we are now getting better at recognizing autism and its range. But while better identification can partially explain the enormous jump in numbers, I also know that it doesn't explain it entirely. There simply were not this many children showing signs of

---

[12] Some epidemiologic studies like those of Terry Brugha of the University of Leicester suggest that the rates of autism prevalence are actually stable but the diagnostic rate has increased due to variable methods of identifying people.

autism when I was growing up or when I was training to become a school psychologist.[13]

When my son's autism spectrum disorder was finally diagnosed, I knew a little about genetics morphing over generations and about potential environmental triggers, but I still wanted to know what specifically caused autism. I had given birth to a son on the spectrum. I wanted to know who or what was responsible. I wanted to know so I could stop blaming myself.

I was thirty-five when he was born, and we'd used a sperm donor—a man several years younger than me—to conceive. For a long time, I would wonder how that particular mix played out.

At two minutes, Matt's Apgar score was 8. At five minutes, it was 10. He was perfect.

As an infant, Matt did everything he was supposed to, but he rarely looked directly into our faces. Babies are supposed to prefer human faces to other shapes; I'd read the studies in college, but for months he explored the outline of our heads. "He's staring at our auras," my partner, Patty, said.

"Maybe he's still connected to a higher consciousness," I said, trying for a joke. That summer at our cabin in the Sierra Nevada mountains, at three months, he would study the bank of windows—a set of six perfect squares—as if he were solving a mental puzzle. Although he smiled at us and laughed and rolled over on time, something niggled at the edge of my consciousness. Something I'd read a long time before in a textbook about child development. Something was off.

We swaddled Matt for six months in the snug burrito roll the labor and delivery nurse showed us, long after the babies

---

[13] Many experts believe a combination of more accurate diagnosis and a true increase in prevalence explains the increasing incidence rates.

in the mom's support group were kicking off their blankets, collapsing into sleep in loose, odd positions in strollers and across shoulders. He eventually outgrew the receiving blankets made for newborns, and when we wrapped him in larger flannel blankets, the burrito wrap did not hold, and he awakened again, crying, too soon.

"He hasn't crawled on all fours yet," Patty told our pediatrician long after Matt should have met that milestone. He had met the others on time. He was babbling, pointing, and imitating the sign language we taught him. "He scoots across the room, but he drags his body with his right arm. We call it the Marine crawl." We had chuckled, but I feared that the doctor would note *delayed motor skills* in Matt's chart. And because of my graduate training in neuropsychology, I also worried that, by not crawling, Matt was missing a crucial step in brain development, and that it meant he would have a learning disability when he got to school. I had read in college about a child with autism being manipulated into crawling motions by four volunteers six times a day to rewire his brain. It was called Delgado patterning, but I couldn't remember whether it had worked.

"Don't worry," the doctor said. "Lots of kids skip crawling." And, as if he has read my mind, he added, "And they turn out fine."

Now, looking at videotapes we made when Matt was a baby, I'm struck by his jerky, puppet-like movements when learning to crawl and when grabbing for toys held out in front of him. As a toddler, he pointed at what he wanted but raised his shoulder and looked over it as if being coy. It was as if he came out of the oven too early, was a little underdone.

One day when he got home from first grade, Matt kicked off his shoes by the door, and I noticed for the first time that he walked on his toes in the house. I had not yet worked with enough children with autism to recognize this idiosyncratic way of walking, which is thought to be an attempt to seek proprioceptive[14] feedback. Matt's arches were so high they were the shape of the monument in St. Louis. Later, when he was jumping on a trampoline, I told him to put his heels down. "Your feet look like a Barbie doll's," I said. Definitely not a Mother-of-the-Year comment.

In college in Indiana, when I first read *Dibs in Search of Self,* Virginia Axline's account of a child she diagnosed with an emotional disturbance and supposedly treated successfully with play therapy, I believed her when she blamed Dibs' mother for his retreat from the social world. I didn't question how the mother's child rearing—which was not unlike many other mothers of the time—would produce such a severely emotionally disturbed child. Now, of course, I look at that case study through a different lens. Even a quick glance at online reader reviews today shows that many others also suspect what Axline simply didn't know because she was a product of her time: Dibs probably had autism.

Years later, during my school psychology internship year, I would work at a public school with an eight-year-old deaf boy who did not use sign language or speech but who communicated with grunts and facial grimaces. He drew picture after picture of the same thing: wires sprouting out of boxes at the top of neighborhood electric poles, connecting houses to poles and poles to other poles. Every day he drew with pencil, crayon, or chalk with such exact detail that he could have illustrated a

---

[14] The perception of movement and spatial orientation of the body in space.

textbook. At the time, my supervisor and I wondered if he had
been neglected, locked in a closet with only a small window
near the top of the wall with a view of the electric pole outside
his home. Now, all these years later, I imagine he was probably
a member of a loving family that was equally confused by his
behavior.

As an undergraduate in Indiana, I took elementary education classes and tutored in a second grade classroom, eagerly
planning to be a teacher. But I grew weary of sitting in my
classes and listening to lectures. I was impatient: I wanted to
get out in the real world right away, I wanted to teach *now*, not
in four years. I was restless and yearned to escape my Indiana
claustrophobia. One day, during the frigid winter of my junior
year, dressed like a polar explorer to walk across campus to
class, I took a detour to the administration building, found the
counselor who had scheduled my classes, and dropped out of
college. All of twenty, I knew I needed to see what lay outside
my little world in the Midwest. Just after Christmas 1977, my
mother drove me to Chicago's Union Station, and, loaded
down with two suitcases, a framed backpack, an overnight bag,
and a macramé shoulder purse, I boarded Amtrak's California
Zephyr bound for San Francisco.

2

Points of Contact

IN THE SUMMER OF 1996, PATTY AND I BROUGHT OUR TWO sons to our cabin for a couple of weeks to let the kids breathe some mountain air, get dirty, and splash around in a small lake every day. One morning, as I watched eighteen-month-old Spencer, Patty set three-year-old Matt on a towel on the sand and began applying sunscreen to his arms. He jumped up and ran off the towel.

"Hey, come back here," she called to him. "We're not done yet."

"I'm finished," he shouted, heading for the water, but I grabbed him around the waist before he splashed in.

"Hey, big boy," I whispered in his ear. From my work, I knew a soft voice could often capture a child's attention easier than shouting. "Get back there to Mama."

"No."

Patty joined us. "We can put it on here or back on the towel," she told Matt. "Which do you want?"

"No sunscreen."

"Yes, sunscreen, but you can pick where you want it."

He pointed to his toes. "There," he said, laughing.

Patty laughed and grabbed him in an embrace, slopping a

few splotches of sunscreen on his arms. When she began rubbing, Matt screamed.

"No sunscreen."

She looked at me for help.

"You have to have sunscreen or you can't come to the little lake," I said.

"I want the little lake."

"Then put on the sunscreen. Come on, hurry up. You're wasting your play time."

"No sunscreen!" he shouted.

"Can we let it go?" Patty whispered. "Otherwise we'll have to deal with a *you-know-what*." Matt had begun, at three instead of the expected two, to throw some doozie tantrums when he didn't get his way. Collapsing to the floor, flailing arms and legs tantrums. Spittle-flying tantrums. Making the dog slink out of the room tantrums. Crying as if the world was ending tantrums. And for what seemed like small insults: the word "no" or even the word "maybe" offended his sensibilities. Answering his questions with "I don't know" could set him off. We would not know for years why he could not tolerate the ambiguity of these answers, or that without predictability he must have felt like he was slipping off the earth.

"No way," I said at the lake. "He's too fair. And we're at five thousand feet." Although at work she kept her public school classroom of deaf students highly structured and was firm about rules, Patty turned to mush when it came to discipline at home—enforcing limits, doling out consequences. "I'll do it," I said. I enjoyed being the strong one at home, not yet aware how this would lead to a troublesome pattern for us.

I held onto Matt's wrist and led him to the towel. "Stand here so your feet don't burn," I said.

"No sunscreen."

I squeezed a dollop onto my palm and began rubbing it onto his back quickly and roughly. He accepted that, but when I reached his arms, he flailed them as if they were on fire.

We'd nicknamed his brother, Spencer, "Mellow Man," attributing his easygoing personality to his status as a second child. We told ourselves we were just anxious first-time parents with Matt, and he simply had picked up on our uncertainties. As a baby, Matt cried every night at dinnertime and needed extra swaddling and rocking in order to sleep. But Mellow Man fell asleep anywhere and woke up happy. Spencer let us rub creamy SPF 48 lotion on his chubby arms and legs, smoothing it on his soft baby skin, sitting on our laps for this ritual. He was a sensory sponge, absorbing cuddling, hugging, and kisses. Spencer often rubbed his cheeks on mine, and sometimes he held on to me as if we were slow dancing, burrowing his face in my neck, letting me nuzzle his. Later, he would smell my forearm and comment on my "rain" scented lotion, saying, "That's your Mommy smell."

"Hold still," I said to Matt on the beach. "We'll be done in a minute."

He shook his arms again, and a large drop of sunscreen landed on my clean shorts.

"Matt, just stop it," I shouted, and his forehead wrinkled in surprise. He began to cry.

"Oh, for God's sake," I said. "Why does it always have to be this way?"

Tears falling into the sand, he let me finish the sunscreen, then ran to the lake and skipped through the shallow water. "Watch me swim," he called, pretending to fall into the shallow water.

"Where did our 'joy boy' go?" I asked Patty. "He's fussier now than he was last year."

"Maybe his 'terrible twos' were just delayed a year, and we're getting them at three," Patty said.

At the end of that summer, I bought the book *Your Three-Year-Old* and searched for advice on handling this little person. I was embarrassed to admit I needed this parenting primer. A school psychologist who didn't know how to handle her own kid.

At three, Matt accepted our kisses and hugs, but he didn't often seek them. When I put my arm around him, he pushed it away. I felt as if I was stealing something when I reached over and smoothed his hair to the side and quickly caressed his forehead and cheeks. When he was sick, he let me feel his face with my lips. I pretended I was checking for fever, but we both knew what I was really doing, getting my kiss fix. He was more independent, and like many firstborns, led the way for his brother, teaching him how to play hide-and-seek and how to host a tea party for their stuffed animals. He had better things to do than stop for "baby hugs," and that was how I explained my son's brushing me off.

On walks when he was a little older, Matt pressed his palm to mine, and every block or so he stopped to readjust our grasp. He needed our palms connected at all possible points and we had to maintain a precise, tight hold. At first, I imagined that it was simply an expression of his love—the tighter he held my hand the more he loved me. But I soon realized it only meant he needed firm pressure where our skin touched.

When Patty or I hugged him while wearing a wool sweater, he squirmed away. "It's too itchy," he said, his face contorted. At bedtime, so he could get his ritual hug, he covered his body with a sheet or blanket to avoid the offensive sweater. When we hugged him without wool sweaters, our hugs needed to be firm. If our vertebrae popped with the pressure of the squeeze, it was an acceptable hug.

At our cabin in the winter, we engaged in a forty-minute squirmy, whiny, complaining battle to get six-year-old Matt dressed for sledding. He didn't wear a coat in winter at home, so the sensation of it on his arms seemed to be a shock, a foreign texture that needed to be repelled, cast off. The wool socks were itchy and didn't line up the right way; the boots touched more of his skin than his tennis shoes did, and he said they felt wrong. The snow pants bunched up in his crotch, and every few minutes he stopped playing to pull it away. It took a few seasons until he could tolerate a knitted cap, and it had to be soft acrylic, not wool. Spencer would be outside throwing snowballs for the dog, but Matt was still inside, in tears, struggling with his clothing. When I lost my patience, Patty took over. Before we all got out the door, we were already exhausted.

When we got home from the cabin the year Matt was six, I looked up tactile sensitivity on the Internet and found the article "Tactile Defensiveness: Overly Sensitive to Touch" and printed it for Patty. *Does your child dislike certain fabric textures, doesn't want his face touched, must have the tags cut out of every piece of clothing?* Matt refused to wear jeans and corduroy pants because the "ridges" bothered him, and he insisted on sweatpants, even when he performed in a piano recital.

Tactile defensiveness, I read, is caused by a neurological disorganization in the brain, in which touch sensations are not properly modulated and cause the child to perceive the sensory input—the feel of something—as extreme and uncomfortable. Matt's brain was registering subtle sensations as extreme irritation, or pain, and he may have been responding in an abnormally reactive way: grimacing and pulling away from the noxious stimulus.

In a neuropsychology class for my doctorate in clinical

psychology, I had studied the central nervous system, the five sensory nerve receptors in the skin: light touch (surface), pressure (deep), vibration, temperature (hot and cold), and pain. The article from the Internet likened tactile sensitivity to cutting a fingernail too short, making the raw sensation of nerves no longer protected by the fingernail almost unbearable. I couldn't imagine what it must be like to feel that way all over one's body, all of the time.

Occasionally, a tag rubbed against my nape, and I had to change a shirt. Did I have a mild form of tactile sensitivity? And did Matt's sensitivity come from me? I now know that we all have varying levels of tolerance, differently formed neural pathways, some more efficient than others. When I was a little girl, I wore scratchy lace dresses, and while I may have fidgeted in them, they didn't make me fall apart over the distress.

There's a funny YouTube video that dramatizes the differences in showering and toweling off practices between men and women. The woman in the video takes her time carefully drying every part of her body, while the man hurriedly slaps a towel across his back and then drips dry as he gets dressed. Apparently, I fit the stereotype since I dry myself slowly and ritualistically. I like to use firm pressure with the towel; maybe that organizes my brain and wakes me up for the day ahead. If I had to pat myself dry or drip dry, the sensation of cold air hitting my body would make me squirm with displeasure.

Temple Grandin[15] built herself a compression box (and later used it as a model for a similar device for cattle in stockyards) to calm her neurological system. Children on the spectrum, we know now, can get relief from being wrapped in

---

[15] Temple Grandin, Ph.D., is a professor, inventor, and author who has autism.

a blanket tightly. Parents quickly learn from trial and error what their children need, whether it's no touch, light touch, or heavy pressure touch. Whether they require no hugs, gentle hugs, or firm hugs.

The article from the Internet said:

> The slightest accidental bump from another person may feel like a threat and he may lash out in defense. It may appear that he is impulsive, hitting others, but no one understands that he is fighting against the perceived raid of his space as interpreted by his brain.

It said that he might dislike group games in which people touch each other and that holding hands can be agonizing. We'd had no reports from his first grade teacher about any unwillingness to participate, but I wondered if she didn't notice him grimacing when she asked the children to hold hands in a circle or line up with a partner, because he was being a good boy. A miserable, but good, boy.

Matt played with friends in preschool, followed the rules in kindergarten, and diligently did homework in first grade. After struggling at the beginning of the year—his teacher had told us Matt was hesitant to make mistakes—he was now reading. But whatever he held in during the day, whatever sensory overload he had managed, whatever assaults to his system he had fended off, it left his coping mechanisms depleted, and at home he fell apart.

I believed it was more than just tactile sensitivity for Matt, though. He had all sorts of nervous habits, habits that I now recognize as his attempts at sensory rebalancing. He pushed his arms straight down onto furniture, twirled a clump of hair on the back of his head, chewed on his nails, and sucked on two upside-down fingers so long that before he got braces, his top teeth jutted out dangerously. "Are we pushing him too hard?" I asked Patty. "Are we expecting too much from him?" She only shrugged.

We hadn't figured out his temperature regulation anomaly yet. At our cabin, we have a photo of Matt standing outside in a snowstorm with his arm around a snowman. The other kids in the photo are wearing coats and hats, but Matt is wearing a short-sleeved tee shirt, shorts, winter gloves, and boots. Our pediatrician had okayed the unique snow clothes "as long as he doesn't get frostbite." Eventually, we found lightweight snow pants and loose, long-sleeved shirts that Matt would accept.

At home, he eventually gave up sweatpants for shorts, which he wore all year. We had mild winters in the San Francisco Bay Area; usually our coldest days didn't go much below forty degrees, but most adults and children wore pants, sweaters, and jackets outside. On the coldest days, kids on the playground wore ski jackets. Other parents at Matt's elementary school teased me when I dropped him off in the morning. We can all chip in and buy your son a coat, they said. I laughed with them, but I was embarrassed. Not because they thought we were neglecting him but because they might have thought there was something wrong with my boy.

He was a paradox. Every winter for years Matt dressed in front of the heater vent in his bedroom, sitting on the floor every morning, pulling on each item of clothing only after warming it against the grate. If we didn't turn the heat on, he would demand it, couldn't get dressed without it. Every spring, when we stopped using the heater, he cried every morning for a week.

In second grade, Matt stopped holding my hand on our walks to school. He was still far from the age where it wasn't cool to show up at school holding your mom's hand, and I grieved this loss. It was one of the first markers of our inevitable separation and it stung. I wanted to hold his hand all day. I wanted to kiss his lusciously soft cheeks. I wanted the contact we shared when he was a newborn and we lay chest-to-chest, skin-to-skin. It was ending too soon. But I eventually figured out that his premature dropping of my hand was not because it wasn't cool but because it was intolerable to him.

When Matt was about seven, he found me in bed at eight o'clock one morning. He'd been up for two hours listening to his headset radio and books on cassette tapes and constructing games with paper. He was quiet and hadn't woken the rest of the family. I took his head in my hands, brought his forehead to my lips and gave him a big kiss, which he wiped off, smiling.

At dinner with my mothers' group, when Matt was six and Spencer four, the talk turned to Kelly's son, Henry, who was having social problems in preschool. "His teacher called us in and told us his social skills were problematic," Kelly said, her voice filled with hurt. "So I'm thinking, lady, this is preschool, we pay you to deal with social problems." Kelly was angry, and I recognized the feeling of being judged as a parent, how our kids are a reflection of us, whether positive or negative. "I mean," she continued, "Don't kids go to preschool to learn how to socialize?"

The three of us nodded, urging her to continue.

"So then his teacher tells us, 'I just read this book, and I think it might apply to Henry.' I was furious. Where does she get off diagnosing my kid? It was so patronizing!" Kelly had a Ph.D. in economics and a high-powered job in a government agency.

"What's the book about?" I asked, hoping this wouldn't make her angry with me. "What does she think Henry has?" I wanted my tone to suggest the woman must be a moron.

"Something called sensory integration dysfunction. The book's *The Out-of-Sync Child*.[16] I bought it. And Henry definitely doesn't have it. We're meeting with his teacher again next week, and I'm going to tell her, 'Lady, you're way off base.'"

"Sensory integration dysfunction," I repeated. It was familiar to me. I had read about it somewhere, but I was fuzzy on the details. "What is it exactly?" I asked. "What does the book say?"

"It's about children who can't tolerate loud noises, certain textures or scents of food, the way stuff feels on their skin, that kind of thing. They also have some behavior problems, social problems, and sometimes tantrums. Henry has those, but not to the extent the book described, and he doesn't have the sensory reactions that they say are the hallmark of the condition."

Something came together in my mind so perfectly I should have been feeling relief, but dread overshadowed it.

"It sounds just like Matt. We have to cut the tags out of his shirts, he hates jeans, he refuses to wear anything but sweatpants or shorts and big, loose tee shirts. Smells don't seem to bother him, but he's a super picky eater." It was the first time I'd talked with them about what worried me about Matt. When we met for our monthly dinners, we usually kept the conversation on our kids' accomplishments, and then turned to complaining about how tired we were and how our partners didn't do enough to help.

Patty and the boys and I were not joining my mother's

---

[16] By Carol Kranowitz and Lucy Jane Miller.

family for Thanksgiving that year because they were meeting on the East Coast. Matt was relieved, but not for reasons I expected, that it was boring to have to sit and talk with relatives one only sees every other year. He explained. "They'll be hugging and shaking hands and everything." He shivered with repulsion.

I hadn't mentioned to my mothers' group the list I'd made of what to tell our pediatrician at Matt's seven-year-old check-up: the socks, the hair twirling, and the full-length mirror on the back of his bedroom door that he'd broken the previous month.

"We definitely have the tantrums," I said to Kelly. "Can I borrow the book? I'd like to see if Matt might have this."

"You can have it," she said, pulling it out of her purse and holding it between two fingers as she might a spoiled piece of meat. "I was going to throw it away."

"This is it," I told Patty that night when we were both in bed reading. She was deep into an Arthur C. Clarke novel, and I was halfway though *The Out-of-Sync Child*. "I think this is what Matt has. At least he has a lot of these symptoms, not all of them, and not as severe as some, but this is the closest explanation I've seen yet."

Patty rested her novel on her lap and peered at me over her reading glasses.

"Especially the tactile defensiveness, listen to this. Reacts negatively to light touch, exhibiting anxiety, hostility, or aggression. He may withdraw from light touch, scratching or rubbing the place that has been touched. That sure is him!"

Patty removed her glasses and twirled them.

"And this, check this out. Fusses about clothing, such as

stiff new clothes, rough textures, fusses about footwear, particularly sock seams. Prefers short sleeves and shorts and
refuses to wear hats and mittens, even in winter, to avoid the
sensation of clothes rubbing on his skin."

"Yep," she said. "Sounds like our boy."

"But there are lots of things he doesn't have problems with,
like forming warm attachments with others, or difficulty in
social situations making him a loner with few close friends."

"But Anne, he only has one good friend."

"He's only in first grade. He made friends with Jake the
first week in kindergarten, and they're still best friends. Isn't it
okay to just have one good buddy when you're six? Some shy
kids don't have any friends."

"I'm just saying that he may have only one friend because
he's having some social problems that we don't even know
about."

"I don't think so," I said in my all too frequent I-know-it-
better-than-you tone. "Look, here's more under the vestibular
system. Poor gross motor skills, clumsy at sports, difficulty
making both feet or both hands work together, such as when
throwing and catching a ball. It's called bilateral coordination,
and it says the child may not have crawled or crept as a baby."

"He didn't crawl, but he crept. Remember the Marine
drag crawl he did?"

"It's him, though, isn't it?"

Patty nodded and looked away.

"At least we might know what it is now, huh?"

"We can't diagnose him from a book."

"But if this is what it is, then it means we're not alone.
And we didn't cause him to be this way. It's a relief," I said,
only partially believing it. Calling it a diagnosis, though, made
it sound serious. Like my boy was sick.

At six-and-a-half, he read first and second grade books, took piano lessons, played soccer. He was clumsy, not as athletic as his younger brother, but he could figure out the Lego kit and put together the model before I finished studying the directions. He made Spencer elaborate structures out of folded paper. One Thanksgiving at our cabin, he made a paper turkey, carving knife, plates, forks, spoons, M&Ms cookies, carrot cake, and chocolate chip ice cream. He wrote me love notes and put them on my bed. I filed *The Out-of-Sync Child* on a shelf in the living room. I was still trying to convince myself there was nothing wrong with my boy.

Before I became a school psychologist, I worked at the California School for the Deaf as a residence counselor, first to accompany the kids on their trip home for the weekend, and later to provide after-school activities for a group of deaf children with mental retardation and emotional problems. At twenty-two, I learned sign language in the back of a long yellow school bus accompanying children to their hometowns —Modesto, Turlock, Merced, Madera, Fresno. Very quickly, I learned how to sign, "What's your name?" "Sit down," "Stay in your seat," "Stop hitting," "Is this your stop?" Then, after several years working at the school, I taught a Red Cross first aid class to a room full of Deaf[17] adults. Afterwards, someone asked me if my parents were deaf. Since children with Deaf parents are native signers, it was the highest compliment. I had become an honorary member of the club, and although I

---

[17] The rise of the Deaf Pride movement in the 1980s has introduced a distinction between deaf and Deaf, with the capitalized form used specifically in referring to deaf persons belonging to the community — also known as Deaf culture — that has formed around the use of American Sign Language as the preferred means of communication. Dictionary.com.

hadn't become a teacher like I'd imagined earlier, I felt as if I'd found my niche.

I visited a friend at Gallaudet University[18] one spring during the Cherry Blossom Festival and sat in on some of her classes in the school psychology department. In those classes, I was excited to learn that I could combine my interests in education and psychology in a career that blended those fields. In 1984, I finished a master's degree in educational psychology, left the School for the Deaf and started my career as a school psychologist in a large urban school district where students spoke dozens of languages, and family incomes ranged from impoverished to wealthy.

One day in the late 1980s, a teacher asked for advice on how to reach a six-year-old boy with autism whose only signed word was "juice." I sat on a kid-sized chair for a half hour watching him match colors and shapes, nest cups by size, and put puzzle pieces together. During free time, he played alone stacking large cardboard blocks, and he cried if anyone moved them. I had been a school psychologist for five whole years, and I remembered my Saturdays at the recreation program playing with the group of boys with autism. But I knew nothing about teaching a child with autism. I wanted to help, but I did not yet have any idea how.

Today's rookie school psychologists arrive on the job with eager and hopeful attitudes, frightened expressions, fierce ethics, and high ideals, ready to save every child they meet. Just like I did. But now, after three decades at this work, I want to warn them about the toughness of the job, how exhausting

---

[18] Gallaudet University is a college for Deaf students in Washington, D.C.

it is, how we need to take care of ourselves and set boundaries or the work can sap the life out of us. But I'm a hypocrite; I don't follow my own advice. I carry work home with me every day. Not papers in a briefcase but scores of kids all tumbling around in my head. I often wake at three or four in the morning and go over in my head what I need to do that day. If I can get back to sleep for a couple more hours, my first thought again when the alarm goes off is always about a student. Many of the school psychologists and classroom teachers I've worked with share similar stories. It takes a couple of weeks into the summer break to finally sleep through the night—deep, regenerative sleep—without waking and obsessing over who needs to be tested, how many reports need to be written, how many meetings with parents are scheduled for the week. During school breaks, I wake up in the mornings to thoughts of gardening and creative writing—and my own kids. When I finally loosen up, I realize just how tightly I've been wound. Sometimes I want to laugh at the eagerness of the newer psychologists. And I'm tempted to laugh at that younger me. But at the same time, I admire her enduring passion.

Recently, two of the younger school psychologists with whom I work independently asked me how I've been able to keep up the pace, the endurance, for so many years. Already they knew they didn't want to work full time at such an emotionally exhausting job. Not to mention the schlepping between schools, carrying heavy shoulder bags, and dragging our test kits, files, and laptop computers around in wheeled cases like harried flight attendants. After I returned from maternity leave the second time, I also lugged a breast pump to work for a couple of months. One day, a male teacher I worked with asked if I'd gotten a new test kit. When I told him what it was, he blushed and nearly jogged away from me down the hall.

I wanted to tell the newer school psychologists how I've tried to cultivate a laissez-faire attitude so all the stress doesn't eat me up, how I've wished I could just show up and do the work and then go home and not think about it. But even after all these years, I can't do it. I do care. Too much maybe, but how can one care too much in this kind of work? Of course we care; it's why we go into the field in the first place. We are a unique breed, those of us in the helping professions.

I've advised my younger colleagues on the importance of balancing work and personal care and how having a creative or physical outlet is important. But I'm not so good at that balancing act. Books about the job of the school psychologist[19] include chapters on preventing burnout and increasing job satisfaction. I've memorized the advice, like learning when to say no, practicing relaxation techniques, and taking a lunch break. But I know very few school psychologists who take a dedicated lunchtime, and we, of all professionals, know better. One of my personal goals is to take ten minutes daily to eat lunch, ten minutes to walk around the block, and ten minutes to meditate, but I haven't been successful yet. Bad habits die hard, or, in my case, hold on for dear life.

When I complained a few years ago about my work backlog and feeling that I couldn't stop to take a deep breath, a sixth grade teacher told me, "It's not a hospital," she said, giving me a hug. "Nobody's dying." It's true I won't kill anyone if I make a mistake, but the way we do the job can significantly affect how kids learn and can have a profound effect on their future. I've been accused by those who know and love

---

[19] *The School Psychologist's Survival Guide* by Rebecca Branstetter, for example.

me of being too earnest. I could be accused of taking the work too seriously, even now, but I can't help imagining each kid's life ahead and how these moments might contribute to those futures. Every time I sit across the table from one of them, I am compelled to do my absolute best work.

And of course there's another reason for my seriousness and perhaps excessive devotion to this work: I can now understand how important this work is to helping the students' *parents*. I am driven by a not-so-mysterious force.

The summer he turned four years old, we signed up Matt for his first swim lessons at the local pool. He'd been in pools since infancy, when we took him to a baby swim class and later when he had played at his uncle's pool. But that summer, with his two moms watching from the bleachers, Matt sat on the top step in the shallow end, and with his palms, rubbed tears from his eyes. We'd seen other young kids cry at swim lessons; they'd clearly been afraid of the water, screaming and clinging to a parent. But our boy sat quietly, stoically, wiping away silent tears. After the first lesson, we took him home and waited another year.

I still wonder if Matt had been exhibiting normal four-year-old reticence, or if the new situation or new people had been too upsetting, or if his swimsuit waistband raked across his skin when he moved. He didn't know how to ask questions, like *Can I watch from the side a little longer?* or *Do you have to hold me like that?* or *Do we have to sing "Motorboat, motorboat" so loudly?* We didn't yet know what was the matter.

. . .

A fourth grade girl I assessed one year wore lots of colorful combinations and layers of clothing that were a few seasons, or years, behind the current style for elementary school girls. When I interviewed her mother, she told me she bought used clothing for her daughter because it was the only clothing soft enough for her. When her daughter was a toddler, the girl had complained one day of "bees stinging" her arms. Later that evening, when her mother pulled off her daughter's shirt to get her ready for bed, the little girl smiled for the first time that day. "No more bees," she said.

Matt and I were walking home from elementary school one day when he wrapped an arm around my waist. My God, I thought, he's touching me; he's showing affection, physical, tactile affection, something he did not typically initiate. I turned my head and stared at him, smiling. We took only three steps like this, and just as I wondered when he'd drop his arm and break the spell, I looked up and almost smashed my face on a street sign pole. With his arm around me, he had been nudging me to the left side of the sidewalk, heading me right into the sign. But I dodged it and gave him a wounded look. He was laughing; to him, it was all a joke. And the sensation of his heavy, loving arm around me immediately faded to nothing.

When Matt was about eight years old, the two of us visited the Humane Society's shelter and tossed kibble into kennels from silver buckets hanging on the gates. "Good dog," we sang over and over. Behind the bars some dogs wagged their tails, some cowered in the farthest corner, and one—a gray-muzzled Irish wolfhound— sat back on her haunches and howled until we moved on.

By the end of our walk-through, Matt had found a dog he loved, settled onto the floor in front of its kennel, and with permission, stuck his hand through to stroke its rust-colored fur. Within minutes, Harold, a Lab-shepherd mix, was pressed to the bars while Matt scratched him behind an ear. Harold's lolling body made him look drunk, and Matt was so relaxed I wondered if he would doze right there on the cold, cement floor.

At that moment, I knew my eldest had a gift, something he could share, a way to entrance a dog by slowly stroking it and whispering in its ear. He was giving Harold a break from the stress of the shelter, and I imagined whatever chemicals surge when we receive and give love were coursing through both dog and boy.

After the required training sessions, Matt and I donned green volunteer aprons and made our rounds. We entered kennels to encourage the behaviors—off, sit, down, watch— that made the dogs more adoptable. Eventually, we walked them to the end of the block, where the boy dogs sprinkled the faux fire hydrant sitting on a narrow strip of grass. One morning, Matt ran two puppies up and down the block until all ten legs were tangled in the leashes and boy and puppies were sprawled panting on the sidewalk.

Many of the dogs were fearful of children, and I loved that Matt could let them experience cuddle time with a gentle child. After we finished more training, Matt was allowed to enter the kennel of a high-strung husky mix named Electra who usually shook in the far corner of her kennel, tail curled between her legs. Matt sat next to the gate and waited for her to approach. Finally, she rested her head on his lap. He looked down at her, his eyes half-closed, he as mesmerized as she. "Good dog," he whispered. "Good, good dog."

3

―――

R o u t i n e

> perseveration *n.*
>
> the pathological, persistent repetition of a word, gesture, or act.

A SEVEN-YEAR-OLD GIRL DREW THE SAME *VEGGIE TALES* cartoons—Larry and Bob—over and over. Every few minutes she stood, held the paper out in front of her, and flicked it with her pencil.

A five-year-old boy stood and flapped his arms as if he was trying to achieve liftoff. When he was really excited, he alternated flapping his arms with brushing his fingers back across his right earlobe.

A four-year-old boy at preschool repeated "truck, truck, truck" over and over until someone gave him the damn truck.

A twelve-year-old girl quoted the lines of her favorite character from the movie *The Little Mermaid* until her mother said, "Time to change the subject."[20]

Matt asked "why?" over and over until we explained to his

―――――――――

[20] Some children with autism begin to communicate via movie scripts. See, for example, Ron Suskind's piece in *The New York Times* on March 7, 2014.

satisfaction, or wore ourselves out trying, why he couldn't have Froot Loops drenched with root beer for dinner.

After upsets, Matt stayed angry with me longer, and he often wanted to talk to Patty, not me. She could get just as angry with him and dole out similar consequences, but when it was all over, he wanted her. He shrugged off my embraces and stared at me with narrowed eyes. At first I thought he wanted to talk to Patty because he wanted to get her to back down and reduce the consequence, but she had stopped doing that when she realized it worked against all of us. She defended me, saying, "Mommy's right; you can't be rude to us." And still he wanted to be with her and not with me, and it tore at my heart. I thought he hated me because I was usually the boss, the dictator, and I never backed down. I was almost as stubborn as he was.

Patty and I were proud that we'd raised our boys to enjoy pesto sauce, made with basil we'd grown. But, like the ducklings that imprinted on a dog at birth, and followed it around as if it was their mother, Matt must have imprinted on pesto sauce the first time he ate it. Because we all liked it, pesto pasta became a weekly dinner at our house. But we could not diverge from the pasta type; it had to be thin spaghetti, or it was "too thick" and Matt could not tolerate it.

Matt also seemed to have imprinted on a specific burrito; it had to be made with refried (not black or pinto) beans and contain only cheese and rice. No meat. No salsa, guacamole, or sour cream. Flour tortilla. He ordered it so consistently at our two favorite Mexican restaurants, the servers no longer asked, "That's all?" His only variety was the size: regular or mejor. At home, he fought changes to our routine meals, balked at vegetables long after most kids give up the battle. We pushed him to try other dishes, but we probably made pesto pasta too frequently. We had no idea of the monster we'd contributed to, the monster of habit. Who would have guessed that we would include a half-dozen containers of homemade pesto sauce in care packages when we dropped him off at college. Talk about perpetuating perseveration.

When I took Matt to see the movie *Adam* when he was about sixteen, I elbowed him when the title character, an adult man with Asperger's, opened the freezer to show rows of the same frozen macaroni and cheese dinner. He smiled. "So?" he whispered. "What's wrong with that?" But when, in a fit of shocking rage, the protagonist (played by Hugh Dancy) swipes a stack of books to the floor and screams at the Rose Byrne character—Matt and I sat silently in the dark theater, staring at the screen.

Whistling Man visited us every few months, jolting us out of the relative calm. Matt woke up whistling. He could whistle on the inhale and on the exhale, God help us. He went to bed whistling. This was not a grandfatherly puttering whistle; it was a noon siren, a train's warning, a call to worship. It was loud and penetrating, and when he aimed for your ear, it hurt. It was happy whistling, though, so I was loathe to complain, but it was distracted, self-stimulatory whistling only pleasurable to the whistler. When I asked him to whistle more softly, he complied, but only briefly, and only after one last great blast.

He whistled without pause for hours each time he rediscovered the habit. Sometimes it was a recognizable tune from

The Sound of Music, like his favorites, "Do-Re-Mi" and "I Have Confidence." But most often he improvised. Sometimes it sounded like he was calling a dog—wee-oh-weet—or inventing a hilly melody that repeated with a slight variation, like a symphony soloist's part. He whistled in his room, walking through the living room, playing on the computer, and setting the table. It was so loud I winced, covered my ears, cried out.

By dinner I couldn't take any more. "Stop!" I shouted. "Make Whistling Man go away."

Weekends loomed. We'd figured out that too much unstructured time—and not knowing what lay ahead—made him prone to tantrums, so Patty and I wrote out schedules for the weekends and left them on the dining room table for easy reference. Before he could read, we drew pictures; later we wrote out lists. Chores, play time, family activity, computer time, special events. So he knew what to expect. By the hour, we laid out the day. He crossed off each item when it was done. It helped. It made us all feel better. Kind of like having a trip itinerary for getting through life.

Matt and Spencer spent hours after school and on weekends playing in our tiny back yard and driveway. Matt made up elaborate and fun games using inline skates, hockey sticks, and soccer balls with specific rules that had to be followed exactly. For years, Spencer tagged along behind his big brother, copying him, obeying his commands. But once he began to have his own ideas how to play games or how to make them up, the conflicts began.

Watching the teachers at the boys' co-op preschool had

taught me more about conflict resolution than my child development classes in grad school had. I used those techniques
when I heard Matt ramping up in the driveway just outside the
window where I worked at the computer. Like a service dog
recognizing the signs of an epileptic seizure before it struck, I
knew the tone Matt's voice took before he blew.

"How's it going?" I'd ask, sticking my head out the window.
"Do you need to take a break? Want some help to talk about
it?" They'd usually regroup and play longer, but if Spencer
wanted to stop before Matt did, Spencer was often held
prisoner for fear of Matt's yelling or threatening to wallop him
with a hockey stick or plastic baseball bat.

"Give him some warning," I'd coach Spencer over the
years, "before you stop playing with him. He can't take the
sudden change."

"I never get a turn," Spencer would say. "It's not fair."

"I know it's not fair, honey," I'd say.

And over the years, I'd say it again and again and again.

At the picture window, Matt waved good-bye to Patty and
Spencer in the mornings, and then with the same hand made
the sign for "I love you" and then waved, alternating the two
over and over. If Patty drove away without giving him the
correct number of "I love you" signs, he whined.

A recent study investigating brain function in adults with autism
spectrum disorders revealed abnormal levels of specific proteins
that correlate with obsessive and repetitive behaviors. I would
have loved to have had a peek at Matt's proteins back then.

•   •   •

When Matt watched videos, he twirled his hair at the back, and eventually a small patch near his crown thinned noticeably. He loved his soft stuffed animals, in particular a lion we'd named Tyre, and while sucking on his first two fingers stuck upside down in his mouth, he caressed the lion's mane with the other three until the poor beast's fluffy aura of a mane was flattened and bare in spots.

"Why is he so nervous?" Patty asked one night as we watched him on the couch.

"I don't know."

"How do we help him?"

For once, I had no opinion.

On a walk with Matt and me years later, our shepherd, Ruthie, stopped and crouched behind our legs. Matt and I spotted the problem. A pair of tennis shoes hung from the electric line across the street, shoes that hadn't been there the last time we took her for a walk, and Ruthie was trying to escape them. We laughed.

"She doesn't like things to be different," I said.

"She's like me," Matt said. "I don't like new things either."

Although I knew he'd shrug it off, I put an arm around his waist and pulled him toward me.

Every night, Matt brought Ruthie's L.L.Bean dog bed in his room where he could lie next to her on his camping mat and pet her until he fell asleep. Often in the mornings we would find her on top of his mat and him rolled onto the hard floor. Spencer wanted a turn with Ruthie, but I put him off. "Matt needs some warning that we're going to make a change in the routine. He needs Ruthie at night, so this will be tough for him." Spencer had gone without, had made more accommodations than any of us, and I wanted him to have the pleasure of sleeping with the dog in his room sometimes. But I knew it would be a monumental battle, and I didn't have the energy for it yet.

Matt's need for Ruthie every night was more than a need for routine, I see now. He pet her so much we joked that she'd have bald spots. But the act of stroking an animal is calming because it releases the feel-good brain chemicals like oxytocin and is even thought to lower blood pressure. Pet therapy. At the time, though, we knew that if we took her away without a lot of warning, a stuffed animal substitute, and a million prayers to the gods of flexibility, Matt would blow up. It was his routine to lie next to her while falling asleep, true, but it was also a more powerful medicine than anything we would ever give him.

Lunch menu
1 peanut butter and jelly sandwich
½ apple cut into eighths
1 granola bar
3 cookies
1 bottle of water

Every day, for years, it was the same. The three cookies—usually Oreos or Chips Ahoy—had to lie flat in their Baggie so they'd fit in his backpack. When I folded the Baggie neatly over them, I found that I, too, liked the symmetry. But when I cut the apple into quarters, trying to move him away from eighths, he objected. You're fourteen, I said. It's time to eat a whole apple. You bite it, see? I pretended to take a nice big bite of a juicy apple. I was pleading for change. But he didn't want a whole apple in his lunch; he wanted a half, and he wanted it cut into eighths. It's fourths or do it yourself, I said, sealing up the two pieces in their plastic bag. Mean Mother strikes again. But he ate them.

On one of the last days of summer vacation at our cabin, six-year-old Matt put on his blow-up ring and swam with me to the dock in the middle of the small lake shared by the home-owners' association. There, we lay on our backs and stared up at the shape-shifting clouds. I mentioned the swim lessons he'd start when we got back home.

"Are you excited about taking them again?" I asked.

"No," he said, "scared."

"Of what?" I was curious whether he was afraid of the water, or having to perform a skill.

"Because I won't know the people." His voice was high with a hint of tears. His face was flat, his lips sucked in.

"I know it's hard to start something new. It's like when you didn't want to swim out to the dock the first time because you were scared, but then you did it and weren't scared anymore. And like when you first went to preschool and didn't know anybody."

"I knew Kevin."

"You didn't know him when you first started. You made friends with him there." I lifted myself up so I was sitting. "You might feel two things at the same time," I said, remembering what I'd learned about ambivalent feelings in grad school. "Scared and excited."

He smiled. "I'm ready to swim back, Mommy."

We stood next to each other at the edge of the dock, held hands, and jumped in.

. . .

IEP, or *Individualized Education Plan*: a document, averaging about fifteen pages long, outlining a special education student's program. IEPs can document students' academic achievement, speech and language skills, motor coordination, health, intellectual ability, information processing abilities, social and emotional functioning, and behavior. They contain yearly academic and behavioral goals for the student, and they outline the special education program that will allow the student to meet those goals. Programs can include specially taught classes in individual academic areas or special classes for the entire school day. Students can receive speech and language services, occupational therapy, technology assistance, counseling for emotional or social problems, and specialized physical education, if needed, in addition to specialized academic instruction.

Because the laws about special education are federal, IEPs are implemented in all fifty states. School psychologists attend an IEP meeting for every student they assess. In a typical 10-month school year, a full-time school psychologist could assess[21] around seventy children, write about seventy reports, and attend around seventy IEP meetings.

    Before every IEP meeting for a single child, school psychologists perform the following: secure parent permission; interview parents and teachers; read the child's cumulative folder containing report cards and standardized test scores; observe the child in class, on the playground, and sometimes

---

[21] For example, by observing the student in class and social situations and administering individual measures of intelligence, visual and auditory processing, memory, behavior, social, and emotional skills.

in the lunchroom; test the child individually over three or four sessions; score tests; speak with private practice doctors or therapists; write a (single-spaced) six- to ten-page (sometimes longer) report; consult with the rest of the professionals who are assessing the student; help write the IEP paperwork; and attend the IEP meeting.[22]

This keeps us busy, and we are generally assessing four or five students at a time, often spread across ages and multiple schools—much like a juggling act running back and forth among three rings under the circus tent. Our calendars are packed with IEP meetings, which are the "performance" part of the job since this is where we present our evaluation results to parents, teachers, and colleagues. Because we are working with several kids at a time, we are always either testing or writing reports. It's a repeating cycle. Astoundingly routinized.

The first time we left Matt at home alone for an hour, he was ten years old. We knew if the house caught on fire, he'd get the dog out and call 9-1-1. He knew the rules: don't open the door for anyone; no cooking; no microwaving; no toaster oven; don't shower; don't play outside; keep the doors locked. I would have bet my life savings he would follow our directions. Matt seemed to be one of those kids who are described as "rule-bound."[23] Rules told him what people expected of him. They let him know how to get through the day.

---

[22] IEP teams consist of the student's parents or guardians; classroom teacher; special education teacher; school psychologist; and other professionals as needed (for example, speech and language pathologist and occupational therapist). Parents are also allowed to bring any professionals or advocates to the meeting.

[23] I first read about this characteristic of many children with Asperger's in *The Asperger's Answer Book: Professional Answers to the 300 Top Questions Parents Ask*, by Susan Ashley, Ph.D.

• • •

One day, when Matt was about thirteen, I changed my computer screen's wallpaper from a photo of autumn trees to one of a bright Southwestern pink adobe house with pink flowers. "Yuck!" he yelled. "Can we change it back? Please change it! It's ugly."

Spencer liked it, saying it was "tight," but Matt could not let it go. He kept begging me to change it until I threatened to cut him off, not let him use my computer at all. I never knew if he objected to the bold colors or simply to the change.

Around that time, the four of us heard the *Monk* character on TV say, "I don't have a problem with change. I just don't like being around when it happens." We all looked at Matt and smiled. "What?" he said, laughing. He knew.

One night, we disbanded at the end of a video, the four of us falling out of our spots on the couch, stretching, Patty and me saying in unison, "Time for bed, guys."

I had forgotten, but those times of transition from one way of being (enveloped by the soft, puffy couch and warmed by proximity) to the next state (standing, moving toward bedtime rituals) often were too much for him. I forgot that this change, this requirement that he make an adjustment, must have felt to him like jumping into an icy lake—a shock that would make anyone gasp. I remembered it, though, each time the tantrums began.

4

———

T a n t r u m l a n d

ONE EVENING, PATTY TOLD FIVE-YEAR-OLD MATT IT WAS
time for dinner, but he was playing with his Legos and
wasn't ready to stop.

"Time to eat, sweet boy," she said. "We gave you two
warnings."

"I'm making a race track."

"You can finish it after dinner."

"No. Now."

"Matt-Matt, dinner's ready. Want me to put it away while
you wash your hands?"

I heard the rise in her voice, which he matched, and I
poked my head in from the hallway.

"No. I want to finish it now."

"It's time for dinner. You can leave it all here until you get
back."

"No!" he whined.

Patty looked at me and shrugged.

"I can help you wash hands or you can do it yourself," she
told Matt.

"No!" he cried, louder. "I'm not finished!"

"Matt, you need to get ready for dinner. This will be here
when you get back."

"No, no, no!"

"That's *one*." Her voice was calm and sure.

We'd found the counting method in the book *1-2-3 Magic*.[24] Three chances and then a time out. It was so simple and straightforward; it was easy to remember, and it helped us stay detached, assume a monotone voice, refuse to get hooked and dragged into the drama. Some of the other parents at our preschool had used it, too.

"No!"

"Time for dinner. We're having mac and cheese."

"That's *two*," I said, modeling what Patty should have said. No discussion, no negotiating. Do it or get counted. I knew the steps, and it irritated me that Patty hadn't memorized them yet.

Patty looked at me. "I need to get it out of the oven," she said.

"Go ahead," I said. "I'll do this."

"Butthead!"

"That's *three*," I said, my voice composed.

"I don't want *three*, you stupid idiot. Poo-poo head!"

"That's a five minute time out, Matt."

That method had worked for us many times. He didn't want a time out—sitting in his room not playing—and usually complied by the time we got to the number two. But at times, like this one, he took it all the way.

"Sit on your bed until the timer goes off."

His tears erupted and he threw his body on the floor, stomach down, head up like a tortoise arching its long neck skyward. He often plugged his ears against our voices, didn't want us to repeat anything; it was poison to him. He splayed his right hand out, palm up, and curled his fingers inward, his gesture of extreme frustration.

---

[24] By Thomas W. Phelan, Ph.D.

I closed his door and sat on the floor in the hall. His cries were sometimes angry wails, but now I heard the intake of breath between sobs coming from his gut as if he was in pain. When the timer rang, I opened his door. He was lying on his bed crying into his giant stuffed bear.

"You don't need to have a tantrum," I reminded him. "You can scribble in your mad book or rip up some scrap paper."

He still could not speak. I knew he hated me when I sent him on a time out, solitary confinement in his room. He didn't say "I hate you" yet, but I saw it in his eyes. And it crushed my heart.

After this meltdown, he was spent. He washed his hands, came to the table, and ate his dinner.

I didn't hold him when he raged, like his preschool teacher had suggested we do and like Virginia Axline did in *Dibs in Search of Self*. I was afraid of "rewarding the bad behavior"—my training in college and grad school was thorough. I understood behaviorism. Reward. Punish. Intermittent reinforcement. Natural consequences. Logical consequences. Ignore the negative. Praise the positive. No debating or negotiating. Stay unruffled. When I was stressed, I fell back on that way of thinking, and it felt both right and wrong. I wanted to kiss and hold him and make it better. But I didn't want to spoil him. He needed to learn the rules. He needed to obey his parents. Who was rule-bound now?

In my master's program, I'd read about authoritative vs. authoritarian parenting. I knew that the former, firm and loving, was the best style for raising kids, and that's what I strove for. But now, looking back, Matt accuses me of being too authoritarian, too inflexible myself, when dealing with him. I believe now that I needed something more than simply tweaking my parenting style—I needed greater knowledge, more help—in order to raise Matt. We needed what I eventually learned through a decade of working with kids on the spectrum. But that came later.

For years, Patty and I argued about how to handle Matt's outbursts. She wanted to give him what he wanted to avoid the tantrum; I was sure that was wrong; we could not give in. But my way felt like breaking a wild stallion. And I didn't want to break him.

During calm times, when I wanted to embrace him, he pushed me away. It seemed as if he couldn't tolerate the feel of my skin on his; it was repulsive to him. When he was raging, I couldn't tolerate him. I didn't want to hold him. I, too, was repulsed.

On his first day of kindergarten, I fought tears as I kissed him good-bye. After lunch, I called him at home from my desk at work.

"It was like preschool," Matt said, and I heard relief in his voice. "We played Lego."

I was relieved, too. I feared worksheets and too much time sitting in chairs. "What's your teacher like?"

"She's like you."

I imagined him smiling. "What do you mean?" I was expecting him to say she played games with us, she hugged me, and she was silly.

"She screamed at us once in a while."

Ouch.

"She screamed at you? What did she need to scream at you for on the first day of kindergarten?"

"Some of the kids didn't do what she asked them to."

His teacher was well respected at our neighborhood school.

She was firm, but I doubted she screamed at the kinder-
garteners. Looking back, I wonder if Matt misperceived her
tone of voice or her facial expression since he was unfamiliar
with other adults' styles. But the fact that he compared her to
me gave me pause. He was definitely familiar with raised
voices.

Recess was short, he said. There were muffins for a snack
and he peed in the boys' bathroom. He would be a good
student; he wanted to please, do what he was told.

"When will I get homework, Mommy?"

At home he cried, yelled, kicked a hole in his wall, but not
at school. At school, he followed the rules, shared at snack
time, danced to music with his best friend.

There was a pattern for us at home: tantrums for a week
or so, then they were gone again for weeks or months. I loved
the peace that followed. I dreaded the end of that space in
between.

One evening when Matt was almost seven years old, I announced bedtime ten minutes earlier than usual.

He checked the clock on his bookshelf. "My bedtime is
eight o'clock," he said, his whine beginning its crescendo. My
gut squeezed in anticipation of what was coming. I had
worked all day, picked up Spencer at daycare, and helped Matt
with his first grade homework while Patty cooked dinner. After
washing dishes, putting away laundry, and supervising baths,
all I wanted that night was to get into bed and read until I
passed out. I was trying to steal a few minutes by getting Matt
ready for bed early, but he had caught on.

"I'll help you get your Pull-Ups on. Want to sing a song
while we do it?" I was careful to keep my voice level. If I

raised it, he'd absorb my frustration and throw it back at me, amplified. "How about the roller coaster song? You have to help me with it because I still don't know all the words; it goes so fast."

"No! I want to go to bed at eight o'clock!"

"It's almost eight now."

"It's only seven fifty-two."

"I know, but you can be all ready for bed by eight. Then we can finish the book we're reading."

"No!" He stomped his foot on the floor like a bull entering the ring, and I knew then that I would need at least the finesse of a matador to get him into bed. I would need all the energy I could summon. I shouldn't have changed the time on him, or I should have given him more warning that tonight would be different. Or I should have just waited until eight o'clock.

But I was tired. Too tired to reflect his feelings or give him choices, too tired to find the patience necessary for that debate. If he had a tantrum now, he'd end up going to sleep later than if I hadn't tried to get him ready a little early. I had interfered with The Routine and now I would pay.

I remembered the advice I often gave teachers and parents at work. *Choose your battles.* If Patty and I fought Matt about everything he challenged, he'd grow up living one nonstop argument. On the other hand, I didn't want him to get his way every time he stomped his foot or raised his voice. And, more importantly, I thought, he needed to learn to be flexible. But I didn't know how to teach him that. And, unfortunately, I didn't follow my own advice that night.

I folded my arms across my chest. "It's time to get ready for bed. If you're ready in ten minutes I'll lie down with you for a few minutes."

"I want eight o'clock."

"I want you to get ready for bed now."

"Why?"

"Because——" I stopped myself. "I've already told you why."

"But why? You never said why Spencer gets to stay up later than me."

We had been down that road many times. I could not engage—remind him that Spencer still took an afternoon nap —or it could go on all night. "That's one," I chanted.

"I want eight o'clock!"

I saw my mistake. What good was a time out now? I wanted him in bed, not sitting on his bed watching the five minutes click by on his clock.

"That's two. If I say three, I will not lie down with you." That was not in the book. Two changes thrown at him tonight. I knew it was a mistake, but my own rigidity had kicked in.

"I want you to lie down with me!"

"If you get ready for bed now, I will."

"But I want eight o'clock!"

He was clearly stuck now, his frustration erupting in lines on his forehead. But I couldn't give in. It would have only reinforced his arguing, I believed, made him more likely to use the same tactics—whining, arguing, stomping his feet—to get what he wanted next time.

"That's three. I'm not going to lie down with you. You need to get into bed now."

He dropped to his knees and pounded his fists on the rug. It had now become a classic textbook tantrum of a two-year-old. But he was turning seven in two months.

"I'm leaving now. When you're ready to get into bed, I'll come back." I was afraid to leave him, afraid of what he might do, but I refused to pay attention to his misbehavior, his drama. Quietly, I left his room.

When I reached the hall, I realized Spencer was no longer

banging his blocks or singing. I hoped Patty was lying on his bed with him. I hoped they were reading a book, drowning out the sounds from Matt's room. I imagined Spencer rolling his eyes and telling Patty, "Oh, boy, here we go again."

Matt slammed his bedroom door behind me and the house quaked. "You're a terrible mother," he shouted through the door. This didn't hurt as much as it did the first dozen times. The sharp edge had been dulled by frequent use.

I had an urge to open his door and shout at him to knock it off, but I forced myself to be quiet. I would wait until he calmed down, then go back and talk to him. But a second later, a crash from his room made me jump. The crash was immediately followed by the creepy sound of breaking glass. A lot of glass. I opened the door carefully as several more shards fell to the floor. A heavy, wooden building block sat on the floor near the door, surrounded by what looked like a glimmering pool of water. But it was a mirage; he had shattered a built-in, full-length mirror that had been on the door for eighty years.

"Get back," I shouted. "Get away from the door. And get your shoes on!" He backed farther into his room, clearly surprised at the force he'd displayed and its consequence. Patty raced down stairs to join me in the doorway. "What happened?" she cried, panic rising in her voice.

Matt began to whimper. "I didn't mean to."

"Look what you did!" I shouted.

Patty left to find the broom, and when she returned and started cleaning up the mess, I stopped her. "He needs to clean this up."

"It's not safe."

"He needs to help."

"He can go get the garbage can in the kitchen."

A part of me wanted him to pick up every shard of glass

with his bare fingers so he would learn a lesson, so he'd never do anything like that again. But I knew she was right. His face was crumpled in fear. It was enough.

"Go get the garbage can," I said, my voice heavy with disdain.

While Patty and I removed the glass from his room, Matt silently put on his pajamas and climbed into bed. Before Patty turned off the light, I removed from the wall the framed photograph of three Atlantic puffins. He would have no glass in his room for a long time.

Patty and I took turns bending over the tiny bed and kissing him good-night. And then we went, leaving him alone in his quiet room, lit by the nightlight glowing softly in the corner, only angry ghosts to keep him company.

The amygdala, a part of the brain involved in fear and aggression, produces adrenaline for energy—fight or flight responses—and it "switches off" the frontal lobe, the logical, rational CEO of the brain, in order to act quickly. I could almost see Matt's bully bulb of an amygdala throbbing and then throwing fierce little amygdala punches when he got stuck, when he raged. I didn't think about what mine must have been doing.

I longed for a magic button I could push to turn the tantrums off. I wanted to smack him; I wanted to yell at him, but I didn't and I was proud of my rare fits of patience, even when he yelled, "You're the meanest woman in the world!"

When I was dealing with a tantrum, my own mother's voice popped into my head. *Because I said so. Don't talk back to me. Do you want something to cry about?*

Like many of my friends, though, I was trying to improve upon my mother's parenting. We had books and support groups now. We knew about reflective listening. *I hear that you're upset*, we said. But I still wanted my kids to obey me because I was the boss. *This is not a democracy*, I sometimes shouted. *It's a dictatorship*.

But still they acted entitled, rude, spoiled. It seemed we parents were stuck in the middle of parenting philosophies: authoritarian vs. indulgent, and the ambivalence was para- lyzing. To help us, Patty and I bought the book *The Explosive Child*[25] and tried the suggestions. But we needed much more than a book could provide.

Once, Matt stood on the ottoman in the living room and shouted across the room, "I am the King of All."

No shit, I thought.

Matt never had a tantrum when we had company, when we hosted play dates, or on bird walks at the Tilden Nature Center on the weekend. We believed he needed to save face. "But it's not fair," Patty said. "If he can control himself then, why can't he when it's just the family?" We knew he held in his emotions in public and felt safe enough at home to let them out all in one loud sonic boom. "We should build a 'get it all out' room where he can go to rage," I said, and then thought of something else. "We could have a sign-up sheet so we could all use it."

After seeing the movie *Men in Black*, I talked to Matt about the alien that took over his body during tantrums. What did the

---

[25] By Ross W. Greene, Ph.D.

alien do with my sweet boy? And how did you get back with us? "Oh, Mommy," he said, his voice full of love. He drew out the Mommy and rolled his eyes so I could see mostly the whites and he looked a little ghoulish. Alien-like.

When I heard him winding up, my belly ached. Anticipating destructive tornadoes is never any fun. We made a plan for Matt. We promised him stars for quiet mornings. Stars for no tantrums. A chart with stars to earn toys from Mr. Mopps' toy store. Some days he woke up smiling when I kissed him. Often it sounded like a calm morning, but we never knew what might set him off. If he made it to the breakfast table without some kind of scene, there was a good chance of a happy morning. We could read a chapter of *Charlie and the Chocolate Factory*, walk to school telling jokes with no clenched stomach, no headache.

"Why can't I read the Palm Pilot manual for my reading hour?" Matt asked me the summer he was twelve.

"Because I want you to read literature. So shoot me."

"But why? Why do I have to read a book? Why?" Matt said, whining. I walked away from him. "Can't you answer my question?"

"I already answered it. No. The answer is no." His dog-gedness still made me so angry I was afraid I was going to have a heart attack or a stroke. Some days I had the patience to glide through his fits of inflexibility, but sometimes I got so angry it felt like my head was going to blow apart. Was it hormones? I was forty-eight, already feeling the slew of body changes. For a time, I believed that was why, at times, for the

most innocuous reasons, I fell into raging fits. Nothing in my
life had evoked such anger as did my children when they dis-
obeyed or mouthed off at me. How dare they? My mother
would never have tolerated what we let slide, and I got angry
with myself for being so weak, not holding my ground, not
being the boss.

This was undoubtedly a time I could have realized this
was not a crucial battle and shown greater flexibility myself. But
I still needed him to obey me, and I had convinced myself that
if I were only stronger, he would. I didn't know any other way.

"I want you to read something besides a technical manual
for reading hour." My voice rose with impatience.

"Why?"

"Because I said so. Finito! We're done now."

"Can't you answer my question?"

"No, I can't." The heat took over my face, my temples
pulsed. "Do you want to wreck the weekend? You are causing
this problem—"

"But, Mommy," he said.

"I'm not finished. Let me finish." We were standing close
to each other, and I kept going. "Do you want to wreck the
weekend now? We've had a good time so far because you've
gotten your way the whole time. You had an overnight with
Uncle Dan on Friday and a play date today. You've been
playing with your new Palm Pilot and the computer, and you
watched a movie Friday night. It's enough. Now, I ask you to
do your reading hour and read something besides the manual,
and you're arguing with me."

"But, Mommy."

"No." I turned to leave. My neck was stiff and sent a dull
ache behind my eyes. I had to get away from him.

"Can't you answer my question?"

"No. Not now."

"Why?"

"Because you're making me so fucking angry." Spittle settled on my lip. "You need to close your mouth. Just be quiet." I pointed my finger at him, and he recoiled into the corner of the couch. I poked his chest. "It's you, you are causing these problems. You need to keep your mouth shut."

"No," he said. "Actually it's you causing it. You're the one making me read, you're the one not answering my question."

That did it. Pushed me over the edge. "You're grounded for the day." Grounding was usually reserved for serious offenses like hitting. I knew it was wrong, but I couldn't stop, couldn't reverse it now.

"No, Mommy." He started to cry. "Am I?"

"Yes." I retreated to the kitchen, and as usual he followed, as if tethered on a line.

"Am I grounded for today?"

"Yes. Get away from me or you'll be grounded tomorrow, too."

He stalked off and slammed his bedroom door. I sat on the couch and cried. This was not how it was supposed to be. I was not the right kind of mother for him. Patty did not emerge from the kitchen; she didn't know how to comfort me. I'd forgotten, too, how to comfort her. It was every person for herself now.

Sometimes, I thought if I let myself cry, I'd never stop. That was what I told myself when I was exhausted, when I could not take on one more thing, take care of one more person's needs. But I learned it was not true that if I let myself cry I'd never stop. Tears eventually stop. Tear ducts dry up.

• • •

A six-year-old boy with a diagnosis of sensory integration disorder arrived at the elementary school where I worked. Nathan had been asked to leave a private kindergarten because he toppled chairs and hid under tables, so his mother home-schooled him until it was time for first grade. I met with his parents and set up accommodations for him. He needed to visit his new classroom before the school year began. He needed to arrive at school early every day to adjust to the classroom before his noisy classmates arrived. He needed a quiet escape when the cafeteria got too loud. In some ways, Nathan reminded me of Matt. His sensory defensiveness and his need for advance warning of changes was familiar. But unlike Matt, he didn't hold it together during school and let it out at home; he let it out in both places. "He can be so frustrating," his mother said during one of our meetings, "the way he has to have things a certain way and freaks out if they aren't. It's so draining." I smiled and nodded. "I know exactly what you mean," I said. It was true; I knew about sensory integration disorder. But I didn't know the whole story yet. Or what to do about it.

When, on the night of a lunar eclipse, Matt called me to watch the last few minutes of the World Series, I joined him on the couch in the living room. As I shifted sideways to stretch my legs, one of my socked feet grazed his bare ankle and he winced.

"Owie. Hurtie," he said in the middle-school baby talk he and several of his friends used. It fit them perfectly. Inside those pubescent bodies, they were still toddlers.

He tried to push my feet away. Because sometimes I just wanted him to toughen up, I left them where they were.

"No, no. No touchy. Better if no touchy."

I dangled my legs over the side of the couch. "Why can't I stretch out for a minute? Put my feet in your lap?"

Just when I thought things were going well, just when I thought we may have had this madness beat, that we were on the cusp of outwitting the sensory integration disorder, just when I convinced myself that he would outgrow it, just when I thought we were past the worst, we were humbled again. Its pull on us, like that of the moon's, was too strong.

The Red Sox made the third out, and Spencer chanted from upstairs, where he was watching in order to avoid a conflict with Matt over couch space or television volume or a million other potential triggers. "Oh yeah, oh yeah, BoSox are the champs."

Matt and I watched a few minutes of the post-game interviews, and then I turned it off.

"Time to brush teeth, love." I wondered if this would be a battle; he was tired and getting over a cold, both precursors to a meltdown. "Let's check the eclipse again, and then you need to get into bed."

Matt clambered like a Godzilla-sized spider to my end of the couch. I braced for his favorite trick—pretending he was about to fall on me, but catching himself at the last minute. I hated this trick because I was afraid he'd slip and I'd end up with an elbow in my eye. But instead he lay on his side, squeezing next to me on the narrow couch, resting his head in the cradle between my shoulder and neck. He was large for eleven, long and burly. His body, only inches shorter than mine, pressed into my side with startling abandon, and his solid torso warmed me. His bare feet, which had recoiled at my touch moments before, were now entwined with mine. His scalp was so near my lips I had only to lean an inch to reach him. His hair, the texture of straw from swimming, needed to be washed, but I kissed his head three times in the same spot, above his temple.

Maybe the dark phase was finally over. Maybe we'd left the worst times behind; maybe he was outgrowing the sensory defensiveness. Maybe the tantrums would end finally. I wanted to believe this so badly, but I knew it was lunacy. At least now we recognized pre-tantrum behavior, could sometimes thwart meltdowns. On our bookshelf next to the couch sat half a dozen books about child development, parenting, and difficult children. Our bibliotherapy.

"Poor thing," I said. "Are you sad because your team didn't win?" I was joking, but he didn't respond. He was the only one in the family rooting for the Cardinals, the whole Series was over now, and it was time for bed.

"No. The Giants are my team," he said smiling. I kissed his head over and over until I remembered this would likely drive him away. Then I lay absolutely still, eager to prolong this moment, his body clamped to mine, becalmed.

"I remember when you were a little baby, and I was lying right here on this couch, and I laid you on my chest and—

"The A's are my second team," he said. "And then the—"

"Come on," I said, "Let me reminisce for a minute. You were only this big." I held one hand at my waist and the other at my neck. "Not this huge ol' long kid you are now."

"Oh, Mommy." He gave me only a moment to hold onto the memory of binding him snugly in a receiving blanket, the baby burrito, and how he sucked our pinkies until they puckered up like topographical maps. "I wanted the Cardinals to win because the Red Sox eliminated the Giants, and the Cardinals haven't won—"

"You always root for the underdog, don't you?" I was grasping his back with firm pressure in two spots, one hand cupping a shoulder blade, the other holding his lower back like a dance partner, bearing down as if he'd float away. Unlike his brother, who sought embraces, I was allowed to touch my eldest so rarely, and I feared each time would be the last. I was careful not to breathe on him.

He rose to one elbow, and for a second I thought he was simply readjusting his position, getting more comfortable, but in the next moment he hopped off the couch and bounced away. "I have to check the eclipse," he said, grabbing his clip-board from the coffee table. Then he left through the front door to draw this stage of the total lunar eclipse, before it began to wane.

5

S t u m b l i n g

A T FIVE, SPENCER DANCED ACROSS THE BASKETBALL
court, the soccer field, and the baseball diamond with
the grace of a gazelle. Ever since he could hold a ball in his
chubby toddler hands, he caressed them, bounced them, tossed
them, and caught them.

At seven, Matt still flinched when a ball came his way.
When we gave the boys scooters one Christmas, Spencer
hopped on and glided up and down the driveway. Matt pushed
once with his foot and toppled over the handlebars onto the
cement. He loved to chomp down on a mouth guard, pull a
bicycle helmet over his head, and grunt when he tackled his
brother on the lawn. His huge grin as he ran on the soccer field
told me he loved it, but he looked more like a lumbering elephant than a gazelle. I remembered the time someone called
me a klutz when I played volleyball in junior high, and I was
determined to protect my son from that hurt as long as I
could.

"I'm really good at sports," he used to say, clueless that he
was one of the least coordinated on his soccer team. "My
sport right now is my bicycle," he said a little later. He saw
himself as strong and fast, which he was, and coordinated and

skilled at basketball shooting and soccer dribbling, which he
was not. He bruised his legs and arms bumping into furniture.
Like me.

Gradually, his little brother began to dribble the ball past
him and sink baskets from farther out. Two years younger,
Spencer was smacking baseballs out of the back yard while my
big boy was still trying to connect the bat with the ball. Over
and over my eldest swung hard, cutting through the air, hitting
nothing. I worried that his brother's passing him up would
break the spell, would cause Matt to realize his limitations,
shatter his wonderful self-confidence. But he didn't appear to
notice.

Over the years, Matt came to prefer blowing the whistle
hanging around his neck and calling time-outs for the family
basketball scrimmages in the driveway. One year, he dressed as
a football player for Halloween, another year he donned a ref-
eree's uniform. He claimed the job of ball boy when Spencer
and I played tennis on the city park courts. And when our
family traveled to the mountains to play in the snow, he piled
snowballs in a pyramid for his brother to throw, then sat and
ate them. My Ferdinand the bull preferred watching to fighting.

We found noncompetitive teams and leagues for both
boys, and Matt's first coaches enveloped him in a cocoon of
acceptance. "Good try!" one soccer coach said when Matt's
kick blasted the wrong way down the field. But as he got older,
I feared his getting picked last, another player telling him "you
suck," or a coach keeping him on the bench for the whole game.

"Do we tell him sports just aren't his forte, or do we
pretend he's a jock?" Patty asked one day as we stood behind
the chalk boundary on the grassy field, the late afternoon fog
sinking upon us.

"I don't know," I said. "I don't want to discourage him, or

make him feel we don't believe in him, but maybe we should cushion the fall, so to speak."

I remembered all the attention my younger brother got for his musical talent, when I knew the music genes had skipped me. I was jealous and resentful. I didn't want Matt discouraged by his lack of sports ability, and even more, I didn't want the difference between the brothers to drive a greater wedge between them.

Matt was a natural at math, drawing, and creating a multitude of projects with paper, scissors, and tape. When he made his little brother paper money, booklets of mazes, and "Keep Out" signs for his bedroom door, Spencer stared at him with awe. Matt had the stamina of a mule; he could hike five miles without breaking a sweat, kayak on mountain lakes like an Olympic athlete, and cross-country ski on intermediate trails for half the day.

One evening at dinner, Matt rehashed that day's soccer game. "Jay and Eric are hecka good," Matt said. "They're the best on my team."

"Their parents played on their college teams," Patty said. "Those boys probably started kicking soccer balls before they could walk."

"And what about you?" I asked. I wondered where he'd classify himself now.

"I'm just good, but they're really, really good," he said.

I loved this answer. At seven, he was beginning to appreciate the distinction, his assessment was becoming more realistic, and the air of nonchalance in his voice told me it wasn't going to be a lethal blow after all. He had worked it out on his own. I had only one more thing to tell him.

"You know," I said. "People are born good at certain things. They have natural-born talent. Others have to work really hard at those same things. You know how Spencer is a natural-born talent at basketball and soccer, and you're a natural-born talent at skiing and art?"

He nodded.

"When I was a kid," I said, "Even though I worked really hard, I wasn't very good at sports. I was usually the scorekeeper."

Incredulous, my firstborn stared at me across the table.

"But Mommy," he said with his brows drawn together like an old man, as if he couldn't believe my naiveté, "scorekeeper is the best job!"

One afternoon, when Matt was in preschool, a telephone operator interrupted my phone conversation with a friend and patched me through to the school. "Matt fell on the slide," his teacher said. "He's okay, but he has a deep cut on his lip." She dropped her voice to a whisper. "Looks like it may need stitches."

I raced to the preschool, remembering an earlier time when I was thirty-eight weeks pregnant with Spencer and I had taken Matt, not quite two years old, to the park. As I watched from a bench, he climbed the slide, heaving his stocky body up each rung, and when he reached the top step, he slipped and fell backwards. It was such an odd image, his falling, like a clip from a surreal movie. There was no apparent reason for his fall. Sand on the steps maybe, but other children didn't fall off the slide at the top, just leaned back and fell through the air until they hit sandy bottom. But like all of the pieces of a puzzle, this one was meaningless without the other pieces.

Witnesses in the park that day will never again see such a hugely pregnant woman move so fast. I was at his side in seconds, bending over him in the sand, waiting for him to move. Being in shock, it took a minute for him to react. Then, once he saw the panicked look on my face, his tears exploded, and he let me pull him to my chest and rock him to the tempo of his sobs.

On the day of the emergency phone call, I picked up Matt from preschool and, while he held a Spider-Man party napkin to his lip, drove him to the pediatricians' office where my boy —who doesn't like to have his face touched, who screams and throws his body on the floor when he doesn't want to do what we ask—lay on the exam table, a hot light shining on his face, allowed a pediatrician he'd never met to inject him with Novocain and sew four loopy stitches into the skin just above the right corner of his perfect baby lip. He squeezed my hand until it ached, but he didn't cry, he didn't wiggle, and he didn't protest. When it was over, he accepted a sticker for each stitch, and another for the shot, and walked out of the office holding my hand.

He would trip in second grade while walking his bike down a ramp, landing on top of the bike and ripping open a large L-shaped flap of skin on the soft, fleshy part of his inner arm just below his elbow. Patty would take him that night to Children's Hospital for fifteen stitches. "He was a trooper," she'd report when they returned. "He watched his arm get sewn up. The doctor couldn't believe how calm he was."

At day camp the summer before fourth grade, the giant redwood log seesaw at the park would come down on the top of his foot, breaking one of the bones. After the first day of a two-week sports camp before sixth grade, he would jam a pinkie playing basketball by himself at home, keeping him out of many sports for the entire camp. He would stub his toes innumerable times. And walking barefoot in our back patio, he'd step on a branch fallen from our lemon tree. He'd land with just enough force to lodge the single thorn a couple of centimeters into the center of his heel.

"What's wrong with my feet?" he'd cry, and we didn't know what to tell him. He wasn't impulsive or into dangerous sports. His younger brother had never been to the ER, and at times Patty and I worried the doctors would accuse us of not adequately supervising our eldest son's activities. We knew it was just Matt's clumsiness, and all we could do was wait to see if he would outgrow it.

After playing on a noncompetitive soccer team for four years, Matt was assigned to another soccer team, one with a new coach and none of his friends. "What's going on?" Patty asked the former coach, the father of one of the most talented players. She listened for a while, thanked him, and hung up the phone.

"He says the team's full this season, that they don't have room for Matt, that he's sorry." Her voice rose. "A bunch of bullshit, it sounds like."

"It's supposed to be a noncompetitive club!" I shouted. "How dare they exclude him just because he isn't a star player!"

"He might get to play more on the new team; it's supposed to be less competitive."

"Less competitive than a noncompetitive team?" I asked. "That makes no sense. They just didn't want him anymore." My chest burned. "We are not telling Matt this."

"What do you want to say?"

"We'll say that the old team was taking it too seriously, and we want him to have fun so we switched him to a more fun team."

Later, when we told Matt about the new team, I studied
his face. I was ready for it to crumple in sadness, or tighten in
anger, but it did neither. "Okay," he said. "Do you think they'll
have good snacks?"

When Matt was eleven, we visited a martial arts studio. He
liked the uniform so we signed him up.

"He sticks out of the pack, doesn't he?" Patty said at
Matt's final testing ceremony. He had worked his way up to
the brown belt test at Kuk Sool Won but still could not touch
his toes without bending his legs, nor could he kick above his
waist. He never broke a piece of wood. He lost his balance
before the others, and he worked hard to keep up with the
complex series of moves. But he didn't compare himself to
anyone else, and he beamed at us when his teacher presented
him with a brown belt in the ceremony.

Soon, though, he realized how many stripes, and how
many months, it would take to earn the black belt, and he told
us he was done. It was a good run, Patty and I agreed.

Shortly after, Matt joined a community swim team and swam
three days a week. His coach taught him how to position his
arms and legs exactly so he could use his strength to its best
advantage and perform the strokes legally for swim meets.
Then he made him do it over and over and over again.

"He's too strict," Matt said, but he was smiling, and we
knew that despite the coach's booming voice and killer
workouts, Matt really liked him. "He's moving me up a group
next week," he said, "because my skills have improved."

One night, Patty told me that when she picked up Matt

from practice, he was smiling more than usual. He bounced to the car, tossed his swim bag into the back seat, and hopped into the front seat. "I'm happy," he said, his voice rising with true joy.

"What happened?" she asked.

"I'm just happy," he said. And that was it.

Hearing this made me feel light, giddy. He'd rarely declared happiness. "The endorphins have kicked in," I said to Patty. "I think swimming is making him feel good emotionally as well as physically."

A few weeks later, I made another connection. "I have this wild idea about the swimming," I told Patty after dinner. "You remember the book about the kid whose parents used patterning to try to rewire their kid's brain? The Delgado method or something?"

She nodded, waited for me to continue.

"I wonder about the swimming. It's so much like patterning when you think about the crawl and backstroke and all of it, all of those laps forming the strokes just right. I wonder if it's been working on Matt's body, easing his sensitivities, physical and emotional. He gets cold sometimes now, or at least he doesn't fight so hard about a sweatshirt. He's had fewer tantrums and he can handle more frustration and he can switch gears a little easier. He just seems more settled and happier lately."

"Or he's just growing up, maturing," Patty said, with the idea that would turn out to be the most probable since Matt would gradually become less and less sensitive to touch as he developed. "Maybe all of this would have happened without the swimming."

"Maybe," I said, wishing she could join my happiness for a minute. "But I like my theory better. A rewiring of the brain.

It could be what gets rid of the tantrums." I knew I was stretching it with the analogy, that it didn't explain everything. But sometimes I needed to grab onto some optimism even if it was naïve.

Patty nodded. "I hope he swims forever."

When he was in sixth grade, Patty and I went to Matt's first home cross-country meet. "Look for me near the back of the pack," he had told us. But during practice a few weeks later, he injured his heel, a bone bruise, the orthopedic specialist at Children's Hospital told us after ordering x-rays and an MRI to rule out fractures and tumors. Matt hobbled around in a boot for weeks, saw a physical therapist for months, and was excused from physical education. But he was undaunted. "I hope I can play baseball in the spring," he said.

6

A L i t e r a l   M i n d

A TEN-YEAR-OLD BOY AT THE ELEMENTARY SCHOOL WHERE
I worked walked along the playground fence, making
several revolutions every recess. He had no friends but was a
strong reader who was at the top of his class in math. He met
with the speech and language therapist for his difficulty with
pragmatics. I had to keep looking up what pragmatics meant.
Language as it is used in a social context. I also had to look up
pedantic speech. *A narrow focus on or display of learning, especially
its trivial aspects.* My computer's thesaurus found: *nitpicking,
hairsplitting.* It was not my area. I didn't know much about
those kids yet.

Patty and I read the boys the *Amelia Bedelia* series because we
wanted to expose them to strong female characters in books,
but we all ended up laughing at her quirky habits and literal
interpretations of words. Who knew that funny Amelia was
probably somewhere on the autism spectrum?

> Me: I'm getting a free ticket for my trip to Maine.
> Patty and Spencer: Cool!
> Matt: What about the way back?

Patty chaperoned a three-day trip to Pt. Reyes National Seashore with Matt's sixth grade class, an exciting overnight field trip and team-building exercise at the beginning of the school year. She and another student's dad slept on cots in one of the boys' cabins. When they got back home, she told me about their raucous group.

"We told the kids lights out at 9:30 and they could talk until 10:00, then it needed to be silent. Matt led the kids in talking, singing, and sometimes screaming. The other cabins were already quiet, but ours was pretty wild. But at 9:59 Matt checked his watch and announced when they had thirty seconds left, then counted down from ten. At exactly ten o'clock he shouted, 'Quiet,' and they were."

During middle school and high school, Matt refereed soccer games for a paycheck. He packed his flags and cards and pencil and coin for the side toss into his duffle bag. He had the rules memorized. It was a perfect job for him. And he was perfect for the job.

"'Get out of my face' means leave me alone," I explained to Matt once.

"But I'm not in your face," he said. "Only the air is in your face."

"I don't have to go to physical therapy," Matt said on another day.

"Yes, you do."

"No, I don't."

"Actually, you do."

"No, I don't."

"Yes. You do.

"I don't *have* to. You *want* me to, but I don't *have* to."

"Oh. I get it. You're right. I *want* you to go."

"Okay."

Matt was reading a book from the library titled *Head over Heels* with a picture of a girl upside down on the cover. He pointed out, "It's not head over heels. It's heels over head. Head over heels is impossible."

I am not terribly precise or concise. When asked simple questions, I provide too much information. If you ask me if I like Brussels sprouts, I'll say yes and tell you I hated them growing up because my mother steamed them to mush, but now I have a wonderful recipe that I got from *Sunset* magazine that uses a lot of garlic and I roast them under the broiler. By then I realize I've been guilty of TMI[26] and I usually shut up. In a court of law, I'd be a terrible witness, a lawyer's nightmare. Just answer the *one* question, they'd admonish. Don't expound.

Even when he was college-aged, Matt would continue to frustrate me (and then become frustrated at my lack of understanding) when he told me something or asked a question without providing enough context so that I could understand his intent. "Just type in 'mission'," he'd say, "so you can get home," making me ask, "What is 'mission' and what do I type it into?" But he'd be frustrated that I didn't understand he was suggesting I use the Google search engine and type in the street where we were shopping. Instead, he used a verbal shorthand that reminded me he still didn't see the forest for the trees. That he didn't quite grasp the big

---

[26] Too much information.

picture when it came to communicating. Or that he didn't yet understand when he wasn't giving me enough information—that I did not know what was in his head but needed him to give me more words. "You use too many words," he'd counter. "But when I use too few words, you don't understand me," I'd say. And after a beat he'd say, "Oh, yeah."

For Spencer's eleventh birthday, Patty and I took two carloads of boys to play laser tag in a nearby town. Despite having the "don't annoy people" talk with him in the kitchen beforehand, Matt talked almost nonstop in the car to and from the laser tag arena. He talked fast and loud and corrected the younger kids so often one of them muttered, "That's so irritating." When one of Spencer's friends called his kazoo a caboose by mistake, Matt waited a few beats and then announced, "Actually, a caboose is the last car of a train." The kid almost threw his kazoo at Matt's head.

> Psychiatrist: Do you know your name?
> Matt: Yes.
> Psychiatrist: What is it?
> Matt: Matt Ross.
>
> Psychiatrist: Do you know what city you're in?
> Matt: Yes.
> Pause.
> Psychiatrist: What is it?
> Matt: Oakland.
>
> Psychiatrist: Do you know the year?
> Pause.
> Matt: 2007.

Psychiatrist: When's your birthday?

Matt: March tenth.

Psychiatrist: What year?

Matt: Every year.

7

———

Metaphor

H E'S A STEAM COOKER. THE HEAT BUILDS INSIDE HIM until his lid starts to rattle and shake, then it explodes off and embeds itself into the ceiling. Then the pot cools, the lid falls back down, and we wait for the heat to build again.

Dear two-year-old Matt,

Lucy had a holiday party for the families at her daycare, and when we arrived she showed us what you had created that morning on the patio. She had never seen anything like it constructed by a toddler. You had placed the six toddler vehicles —tricycles, push cars, and scooters—in a large circle. Next to each of them you stood a foot-high redwood post. We asked you what it was, but you didn't say. It reminded me of Stonehenge and also of one of your tea parties and how you seat your babies in a circle and give them each a plate, cup, and spoon. This pleased me because it shows you were developing 1:1 correspondence, which will help you when you learn math. But, still, I wonder what you were thinking when you built it. What it means.

Love, Mommy

Now I think of Temple Grandin, who taught us how people with autism see the world, often in pictures with a particularly strong understanding of visual systems. She almost failed algebra but aced geometry. I recently tested a seventh grade boy with Asperger's who told me that in order to remember information he saw pictures in his head. Some students I've worked with who are on the autism spectrum have difficulty understanding figurative language like idioms and metaphors, and some show limited imaginative play. But not all. And not Matt.

The first time Matt saw a football tackle and pileup on TV when he was about two, he laughed and said, "Whole family fall down." And the first time he witnessed a football huddle, he said, "Kiss, hug." Patty and I loved this so much, and we would tell him this story so many times he'd finally—around sixteen—beg us to stop.

After I showed him how to give "fish lip" kisses (with puckered lips) when he was about six, he said, "Fish lips are like the inside of a kiwi." Around that time, his foot fell asleep, and he said, "It feels like there's sand inside my foot." I knew his language development was simply typical for his age, but to me, he was Harvard-bound.

In the bathtub when he was in preschool, Matt dictated stories about a moose and a fish diving into bubbles and throwing soapy water on a tiger. When he went to sleep, I typed them up and printed them in 16-point font. We used a three-hole punch and placed them in a binder. They became bedtime stories. Super Mom encouraging her child's literacy.

Later, we started mutual storytelling. I didn't interpret but just let the stories flow. Super Mom using her training in psychology. "Who's in the story?" I asked one night. "A monster," he said. I made it a growling, chasing monster. He corrected me. "She's supposed to be a friendly monster, Mommy." That brought Super Mom down a notch.

We didn't yet know about Carol Gray's Social Stories books,[27] which Patty and I, both educators, would have jumped all over to give Matt another way to help him figure out what people expected of him, what was coming up in his day, and to review social situations that had gone poorly or particularly well. They might have prevented a meltdown or two. But maybe reading almost every *Berenstain Bears*[28] book written was our version of Social Stories; perhaps along with millions of other kids, our boys learned more than a few manners, morals, and social cues from hearing how the Berenstain Bear family handled their dilemmas.

Seven months pregnant with Spencer, I lay on the couch after work while Patty cooked dinner and I watched twenty-month-old Matt. I tried to doze, but Matt wanted to "feed" me from his play kitchen—a low bookshelf with stacks of plastic dishes and utensils. He served me "appa cake," and when I pretended to spill it, he giggled. When I pretended to throw it at him, he laughed and imitated me. We got so raucous, Patty came out from the kitchen to see what was going on. Matt pretended to throw a piece of "appa cake" at Patty, and she joined the food fight, all of us ducking and shrieking as imaginary apple cake hit the walls. We were so happy in the womb of our family. Our ordinary family.

---

[27] Social Stories (*The New Social Story Book* and *Comic Strip Conversations*). A Social Story describes a situation, skill, or concept in terms of relevant social cues, perspectives, and common responses in a specifically defined style and format. The goal of a Social Story is to share accurate social information in a patient and reassuring manner that is easily understood by its audience.

[28] By Stan and Jan Berenstain.

• • •

One day after preschool, four-year-old Matt rolled up in a ball and squeezed onto my lap. "I'm your baby, Mommy. Pretend."

"Okay," I said. "You're my baby." I stroked his face and pushed his hair back behind his ears. "Here, baby, here's your bottle. Now I need to change your diaper, your poopy diaper." I tickled his side for a second and pretended to change him.

He laughed. "Change me again."

Then two-year-old Spencer walked into the living room, and Matt's eyes became narrow gashes. "Don't talk to him," he said, stretching out across my lap. I remembered this feeling of life-threatening rivalry as a kid. Our family seemed so typical, so ordinary. Most of the time.

As soon as he could write all the letters in the alphabet, Matt asked us, "How do you spell 'I love you'?" Next, he constructed paper mailbox pouches and taped them onto the bedroom doors. *MoMMyS mailbox*, mine read. Sometimes he ran into the living room with a pleased grin. "Have you looked in your mailbox?" Delivery was sporadic: some days nothing appeared in my pouch, other days there were three batches in a single afternoon.

At some point the mailboxes disappeared, and then we received hand-delivered messages: pencil on brown construction paper; purple marker on yellowed onionskin; and crayon scrawled on the back of my grocery list. When he began to take showers in the morning, he even wrote the love notes with his finger on the steamy bathroom mirror. Eventually the notes left on my placemat lengthened. "Mommy I Love you will you Please Take us to Toy Go Round?"

During a family meeting one evening to remind the boys yet again that bathroom talk was not allowed at the dinner table, I expressed my frustration. "I just want a peaceful dinner!" Ten minutes later a note appeared on my pillow. "I'll try to be better next time MoMMy. I'm sorry you felt bad. I love you from Matt."

One evening during a battle over piano practicing, Matt said something that made me burst into tears and leave the room. Five minutes later, he hand-delivered a note written in pencil on a piece of clean computer paper, folded into quarters. I opened the note, not knowing what to expect.

"I am Sorry That I said I Need a New mother. I Love you. ☺"

Shortly after, I received one more note that I would save forever. It was my badge of being a good mother, and I'd keep it for all the times I acted like a crappy one. Completely unexpectedly one night, when I was listening to Spencer reading on the couch, Matt slipped me another message. This one was written in pencil on a torn corner of pink construction paper. While listening to *Hop on Pop* I unfolded it and snuck a peek.

"I Love you MoMMy. you'r tite, cool and you rock, from Matt."

One day, I put my arm around Matt and squeezed him hard and did it quickly before he could pull away. "How did you get so cute?" I asked him, smiling at him and feeling deep mother love. He smiled back at me. "It must have been the sperm donor," he said, chuckling at his own wit. I punched him on the arm. "You meanie," I said, laughing.

• • •

A week before Pi Day (March 14), Matt was memorizing the first fifty digits of pi for a contest in his math class. The student teacher in seventh grade algebra had promised to buy a pie for the student who memorized the most digits. Matt printed out the first one hundred digits and carried the paper in one of his pockets. He added the first six pages of pi numerals, single-spaced, to his bedroom door. When we knocked, he demanded we read a few lines to gain entrance. He stayed in his room studying, talking into his voice recorder, and playing it back. "How do you do it?" I asked him when I tested him the first time and he recited twenty numbers. "I clump some of the numbers together in groups," he said. "Chunking," I said, recalling the memorizing technique from my psychology training. "Good for you."

But it was freaky to hear him recite a string of random numbers as I checked his progress. He could rattle off twenty, and then thirty. "Who else is competing in this contest?" I asked him, picturing him as the only one, looking more than geeky when he stood in front of his class reciting numbers in a monotone. I feared it would ostracize him, make him freakish. But he said half the class was trying it.

"*Why* do you do it?" I asked. "For the pie, of course!" he'd said. But I wondered if it was because he was comfortable in the realm of numbers and he had found his place. "I think Pi Day should be a national holiday!" he said.

On March 14, he left home for school to our cheers, "Go Pi Day! Win us a pie!" He knew fifty digits, but he was afraid he'd get off track somewhere along the line, that nerves would make him forget one sequence.

After school, I picked him up for an orthodontist appointment. He got into the car quietly, not thrilled to be getting a second set of braces.

"Well?" I asked.

He glanced at me. "What?"

"Well?" I waited. "Did you win us a pie?"

"No." He smiled. "No pie for dessert."

"Darn!" I said. "Did you forget? Or say the wrong number? Did she let you take it back? Who won?" I have a bad habit of asking questions on top of questions when I'm excited.

"Sam."

If his friend Daniel had been in his class, Matt would have lost, too, because Daniel knew eighty-some digits, which he could rattle off like a machine. I was beginning to understand what those boys enjoyed about each other, why they were compatible. Their brains worked alike.

"How did you do?"

"I came in second."

"Wow!" I shouted as we pull away from the school and headed to the orthodontist. "You did great! Second place. How many kids competed?" I feared it was just the two of them, Sam and Matt.

"About twelve or thirteen."

"Fantastic!" I said, relief turning me practically manic. "After the orthodontist, I'm buying you a pie!"

8

T r e a t m e n t

There are significant concerns regarding Matt's sensory processing skills; he is displaying signs of sensory defensiveness, which is thought to be caused by a difficulty modulating sensory input in the brain. A child with sensory defensiveness may react to "normal" levels of sensory input with a defensive fight, flight, or fright reaction. He also shows difficulties with emotional regulation, and sleep-wake cycles. He also has difficulties with temperature regulation. It is felt that Matt's sensory processing difficulties are having a significant impact on his quality of life and behavior at home.

OUR INSURANCE COVERED THE OCCUPATIONAL THERAPIST'S evaluation, which confirmed what we were struggling with—that Matt's behavior was caused by neurological "miswiring." But that's where the insurance company drew the line. They would cover none of the recommended treatment— weekly visits to the occupational therapist to swing and spin on twirly objects, listen to modulated music, and receive joint compression[29] or other methods of organizing and calming the neurological system. We'd heard this was typical of insurance

---

[29] Done in a particular way and in a particular sequence under the supervision of an occupational therapist.

companies in the late 1990s and that it was not worth fighting. We started writing checks.[30]

Using a soft surgical scrub brush—plastic and a little larger than a fingernail brush with soft, flexible bristles—I stroked Matt's arm in the prescribed manner.[31] Down and up its length from shoulder to wrist, counting out a minute on this column of flesh before moving over a few inches and repeating the motion on another. It was heavy pressure, and this he tolerated; it was my other hand lightly grasping his elbow, holding up his arm and keeping it firm and straight, that irritated him.

"Don't hold my arm!" he complained. "Don't touch it." But it felt as if I was brushing something in space; there was so little resistance it seemed his arm would go floating off into the void if I didn't hold it.

"I need something to push against," I said. "Can you keep your arm straight for me?" He straightened it and pushed his palm against my thigh, and I finished his arms and moved to his back, and then his legs. Up and down from his upper thigh, over his shorts, to his ankles, to the tops of his tennis socks.

This ritual, which Patty and I took turns performing every two hours during the day, beginning when Matt was seven, encouraged his nerves to reorganize, to tolerate more stimulation. Or so we had been told. Maybe in twenty years it would be deemed as archaic as leeches. I thought of the now discredited practice of phrenology, imagined myself running

---

[30] Since about 2008, state legislatures have begun passing laws requiring insurance companies to provide autism-related therapies (for example, physical, occupational, speech, and applied behavior analysis).

[31] Developed by Patricia Wilbarger, M.Ed., OTR, FAOTA.

my hands over my son's head to map it. Next we'd be testing the "humors" of his body. The brushing looked so strange, like some kind of medieval torture; I was careful to draw his blinds before the bedtime brushing so our neighbor wouldn't witness it, so we wouldn't have to explain. When we finished brushing each limb, we pushed against its joint, as if encouraging the arm or leg back into its socket. It was an intimate process, but I felt oddly disengaged. It was how I was allowed to touch my son.

I wrote out a daily schedule, both for the brushing and for a listening program recommended by the occupational therapist. We had purchased modulated music on CDs—mutated Mozart and Carulli—which Matt now listened to several times a day over a one-hundred-dollar headset we'd bought for this purpose. I'd made enough copies of the schedule to last us a month, so we could check off each day's sessions. It was the summer between first and second grades, so he listened to music in the morning, afternoon, and before bed. And every two hours we pulled out the brush. I carried one in my purse; Patty carried one in the back pocket of her jeans.

It took about five minutes once we got the routine down. He sat on his bed or the living room couch, we asked him where to brush first, and then we moved systematically over his body until his limbs and back had been stroked, awakened, desensitized. No belly, no head or neck, for brushing those areas would disturb his neurological functioning, we were told. *As if it isn't disturbed now*, I thought.

Five-year-old Spencer watched us brush his brother, saw how much time we spent touching Matt when he didn't even want it, how we begged Matt to stop playing and accept another brushing. It must have been so odd for Spencer, a child who loved to be touched. How did he understand all of this? "Want me to brush you, too?" I asked him, hoping I was not offering something that would impair his adequately functioning sensory system, turn his nerves wacky. He accepted and a couple of times I brushed him, holding his ropy arms, so unlike his brother's thicker, more substantial ones, so he could feel what it was like. But he lost interest quickly, realizing it took time away from play, and he preferred hugs and kisses throughout the day and bedtime cuddling anyway.

It started like all the rest. At breakfast, Patty told seven-year-old Matt he needed to hurry up, and he took it literally. "I don't *need* to hurry up, you *want* me to hurry up," he said. "*Need* is not the same as *want*." When I tried to teach him the finer, more abstract meaning, he pressed his palms to his ears. But I pushed, said he was being rude, that he needed to listen to me. The first explosion came almost immediately.

"Shut up, Mommy! Just shut the fuck up!"

"Go to your room, Matt," I said. "Go calm down."

"I *am* calm!" he shouted.

We sometimes went months without a tantrum, and I slipped into complacency, teasing myself with the idea that maybe they were finally gone, that he had finally outgrown them. But when Matt slammed his fist into a framed picture in the living room, we realized the giant had only been sleeping. And when it awakened, and I raised my hand to slap him, I knew we needed help.

The family therapist's walls and shelves were covered not with diplomas but with Star Wars posters and memorabilia. The therapist himself looked amazingly like Chewbacca with his long silky hair and goatee. The knickknacks outnumbered the professional texts in his small office, but I did notice the thick, dictionary-like *DSM-IV*,[32] the diagnostic reference text, in a prominent place on his desk, the only visible tie to his profession. We had driven ninety minutes to see him, and I was relieved to have found his office without difficulty, relieved that Matt didn't get nauseated in the car, and relieved to be sinking into the leather couch. Patty and I sat on either side of Matt. I hoped the therapist noticed that our boy was between us, and I wondered if he would interpret both contexts. That this boy was loved and included and also that he divided us.

It was important to me that this therapist was not a psychoanalyst, and it looked as if this man's god was Yoda, not Freud. During my own studies in a clinical psychology doctoral program that taught a range of psychological disciplines— from Freud, Jung, and Klein to the family therapists Satir, Minuchin, and Michael White—I aligned with the latter group. This Wookiee warrior look-alike practiced Brief Therapy, a method I appreciated because of its effectiveness and the way it shouted at conventional Freudian therapists, *See! You don't have to be in analysis for ten years to get better!*

I had interned as a family therapist when working on my doctorate. I loved helping families with out-of-control teens and preteens learn how to talk to each other and fix their broken system. I wondered how this family therapist would view us and had to trust he would not make too much of our two-mom family and not blame Matt's having two mothers and no father for the cause of the tantrums. I had told him on the phone that it was important Matt not be identified as the problem, the "identified patient," as it's called in the therapy field.

---

[32] The fourth version of *Diagnostic and Statistical Manual of Mental Disorders*, published by the American Psychiatric Association.

Children's behaviors are often a reaction to their family's functioning as a system. It is often the parents who need the therapy or parenting guidance, and once they are on an even keel, the children will follow. I still believe in this for families with neurotypical[33] children. Therapists working with families who have children on the autism spectrum, however, need additional knowledge about the neurological and sensory differences that explain many of the behaviors of a child with autism. Despite my preference for short-term therapy, when we arrived at the family therapist's office, I was willing to work with Patty for as long as it took.

"Why don't you tell me why you've come?" he said, raising his legs and resting his Converse sneakers on the leather ottoman connected to his leather lounge chair. Patty and I launched into the history of the tantrums. We were paying him $195 for this first session, which would last an hour and twenty minutes. Once again, our insurance would not cover it. We mentioned the tactile sensitivity, auditory defensiveness, how Matt got overwhelmed, overstimulated, how all the built-up feelings came boiling out, and how eventually he returned to our calm, sweet boy. I made sure he didn't think we rewarded Matt in any way for the tantrums, that none of us were enjoying them or getting any secondary benefit from them.

The therapist leaned forward in his chair. He took no notes, just asked a few questions of us and Matt.

"I agree with you that Matt has some control over the tantrums," he finally said. "He needs to get total control over them. Do you agree, Matt?"

Matt nodded. He had been quiet in his wide-eyed, intimidated way.

---

[33] Neurologically typical (as opposed to autism, which is considered neurologically atypical).

"I want you to control the tantrums for one week. If your parents tell me next time that you controlled the tantrums, I will pay you five dollars."

Matt smiled for the first time. His glance at me said, *Is this guy for real?*

I wondered what kind of intervention this was. It didn't feel right; it was an oversimplification, like he hadn't heard anything about the sensory defensiveness, the getting stuck, perseverating on topics, Matt's rigid thinking. At first I was angry. Why don't you just recommend a *Star Wars* trilogy boxed set to fix those tantrums?

But I knew he was externalizing the problem, giving us a test, trying to determine how and when Matt could control his outbursts. I thought he'd reframe the tantrums, suggest that they functioned to get Patty and me to engage. I wanted to tell him the tantrums did indeed make us engage. We usually ended up fighting over how to handle them. We were all quite engaged—yelling at each other. Then came disengagement, pushing each other apart.

We were quiet on the long drive home, but that night Patty and I whispered to each other in our room.

"It sounds more like a bribe to me," I said. "We paid $195 for that?"

"Don't forget," Patty said, feigning seriousness, "we'll get five of that back."

We continued the brushing, just three times a day now. But Matt rejected it, pushed our hands away, and we stopped. He listened to the modulated music, now it was prescribed like a controlled substance, starting with five minutes once a day and adding a minute every fourth day as long as no "intense behavioral or emotional reactions occurred." As if we had no experience with intense behavioral or emotional reactions.

We did exercises from the Brain Gym[34] therapy: gave him crunchy food, let him drink everything through a straw, encouraged him to use the pull-up bar we installed in his bedroom doorway. The occupational therapist at the clinic talked with Matt about his "engine speed" and how to increase it and decrease it. Together they made a colorful cardboard dial with a moveable arrow, like a fire danger sign, so Matt could show us how revved up his body felt. We made him a stress ball by filling a sturdy balloon with flour and tying it securely. It broke within a week because he bit it while watching videos, and flour spilled over him and into the creases of the couch. I bought him a stress ball from the office supply store, and he kneaded it like a chunk of dough. The Zen of Brain Gym.

When he was about eleven, Patty and I wanted to know if there was a medicine that would help Matt with the tantrums. They still crept up on us, taking us by surprise, and we reacted like a veteran soldier might to a car backfiring. Maybe there was a magic potion that would make them disappear.

At first, our insurance company couldn't find us a child psychiatrist in our Bay Area town, which was like not being able to find an apple at the fruit market. I had made my way down the list from the HMO, calling twelve psychiatrists within a ten-mile radius. No openings. On vacation. No longer practicing. Never heard of sensory integration disorder. Doesn't see children. Doesn't take that insurance anymore. I called the HMO again. Got another list.

---

[34] Learning through movement.

Later, when Matt went to middle school, we brought him to a clinical psychologist who met with a group of sixth grade boys to work on social skills. She taught them to recognize facial expressions and to navigate social situations. But because she was not on our HMO's list, we had to fight for approval, then for reimbursement.

At work, when I referred families to therapy, I'd been astonished at how many never followed through. Was it fear? Denial of the problem? If they didn't have insurance, they had Medi-Cal, so what was the problem? I was beginning to understand.

The psychiatrist our insurance company approved when Matt was eleven ushered us into her office in her home in San Francisco. A young Irish setter ran out and jumped on all of us in turn. "Lester! Off!" the psychiatrist ordered without effect. "Do you like dogs?" she asked. *If they don't jump on me*, I thought. *If their owners can control them.* The three of us nodded solicitously, and the dog accompanied us into the office, a long, narrow room frozen in the sixties. The walls were papered in a bamboo print, and fringe swung from the lampshades.

The dog was too frisky, sniffing crotches, testing our tolerance by placing a paw on the couch we three were sitting on. I raised both hands several times in the *I give up* gesture, but Matt didn't seem to mind. He laughed when the dog nudged his head under Matt's arm. Finally—I would have acted much sooner—the psychiatrist grabbed the pup by the collar and dragged it out of the room. "He's cooped up in the kitchen most of the day," she said. "He loves to get out and socialize." It sounded as if she was trying to make me feel guilty for not allowing him in my lap.

When she returned, she ran through questions from a

sheet of paper and took notes in a file folder with Matt's name on it. We had come to talk about medicine, its pros and cons, side effects, efficacy rates, but she began scribbling on a prescription pad while telling us that Prozac was working wonders on children with explosive issues.

I had been hoping for an anti-anxiety medication and didn't understand why she was prescribing an anti-depressant. It was his anger we needed help with. And I had just read an article in the paper about teenagers becoming suicidal while taking Prozac, but she pooh-poohed the report and called it unsubstantiated.

We had to trust her. We had no one else to go to unless we paid out of pocket. It had taken four weeks for the insurance company to give us an authorization and another two weeks to get an appointment. She had been practicing a long time, but I wondered if she stayed current with the research literature. By the look of her cluttered office, she was still catching up on journals from the seventies.

Patty took the prescription from her. I didn't want to touch it. Now I finally knew what it might have been like for the parents to whom I'd suggested getting a medication evaluation when their kid showed signs of an attention deficit. I didn't want to give my baby a powerful, scary drug. Did he really need it? Would it hurt him? Would it change his wonderful loving personality? Would it help with the tantrums, the main reason for trying it?

When Matt had an outburst, or got so illogical I felt as if I was going crazy, I was ready to pop some pills myself, but the Prozac side effects were scary for an adult, so how could I consider giving them to my child? Nausea, headache, trouble sleeping, dry mouth, dizziness, rash, itching, trouble breathing. TROUBLE BREATHING! What the hell were we doing?

"It feels like cheating to medicate him," I said to Patty. "Are we just being lazy? Maybe we should work harder, try therapy longer."

"He's sad," she said. "He cries more than he laughs lately, especially after a tantrum."

I knew she was right, but once the pills were sitting on the counter, I felt as if we had failed. When Patty broke open the capsule and mixed it in his apple juice, I was ready to cry. When he drank the first few sips, I had to leave the room.

"He's in a good period now," I said to Patty a month later. "The boys are bickering, but we haven't had any tantrums." Our winter vacation at the end of 2004 had been wonderful; the boys were playing hockey on skates in the driveway and the four of us had gone to movies and a Cal basketball game together. My mother and brother came for dinner on Christmas, and as soon as we finished eating, we excused the boys to play with their new Lego kits while the adults stayed at the table to talk. The presents we dubbed the Lego Dinner Saver.

"I want to stop the medicine," I said to Patty in January. "I can't stand giving it to him. He doesn't need it."

"We haven't given it a chance," she said. "We need to give it more time to see if it works."

"But even before we got the prescription, things were better. No tantrums. Just normal kid stuff. How can we tell if the medicine is working or if it's not doing anything at all?"

"The tantrums will come back, and we'll have to start him on it again."

"Maybe they won't come back. Let's think positively."

"Let's be realistic, Anne."

"I just can't do it to him," I said, aware that it was me I was protecting, too. I took the medicine bottle from her and placed it on the top shelf of the pantry behind the cayenne pepper.

9

Normalcy

SOCCER AND LITTLE LEAGUE, GYMNASTICS CLASSES, PIANO and trumpet lessons, cross-country skiing, ice skating in San Francisco. Horseback riding in New Mexico when visiting grandparents. Legoland and the San Diego beaches. Disneyland. Block parties and lemonade stands on the corner. Sitting on Santa's lap.

Matt and I took a cross-country skiing "skating" lesson one winter in the Sierras. He caught on quickly, and after lunch we skied fast, challenging each other and laughing on trails we had almost to ourselves. Times like these I wanted to shout to the snow-covered peaks, "Why can't it always be like this?"

When Matt and I picked Spencer up from preschool, Matt gave Spencer one of his crackers. Another mother put her hand on her heart. "Isn't that sweet?" she said.

There were moments when Matt flashed me looks of pure disdain, like I did at my mother when I was thirteen. He refused to shower or wash his hair, or he bickered with me on walks, complained about everything, asked over and over when are we going to be there? Do we have to walk? Can't we drive? Aggravated, I told him to chill, but then I realized what he was doing was normal preteen behavior. Normal.

Nine-year-old Spencer stomped to his bedroom shouting about what "parental idiots" we were because we had sent him to his room for calling his brother a dickhead. Although Matt's tantrums sometimes made Spencer cower in his room, Spencer could get Matt raging by promising to play with him and then reneging or by calling him "Fat Ass." But he was angry with us when we gave him consequences. "You're the worst parents I've ever seen," he shouted from upstairs. "You need to take a parenting class!" Patty and I exchanged smiles. I stifled a maniacal laugh; the irony was perfectly hilarious.

Lying on the couch one winter during elementary school, Matt ate a few Saltines dipped in Sprite, and slept for two days. On the end table next to him sat a box of tissues, a trashcan, and a stack of unopened books. His face was flushed, angelic, and he huddled under two fleece blankets with two bed pillows under his head. Then, one evening, he began shouting for pesto pasta from his reclining throne, his returning hunger and the volume of his voice telling us he was getting better. It was the quiet that disappeared. The quiet that was, for a brief period, a sanctuary.

The summer after Matt's fifth grade, we split up the family for part of the vacation—one mom and one kid, then a switch. I joked to friends, "I *live* with these people, why would I want to vacation with them?" and laughed the hardest, believing my joke for a long time. I did love our splitting up, enjoying one boy at a time, and wondered why more people didn't do it. I began to feel superior because of this knowledge—separate vacations were peaceful. Who needed the fatigue of travel and the bickering all families do when they're spending every hour together? It would be several years before I realized what we were missing. Taking a family vacation can be peaceful; it can be a way to share enjoyment with one's children in new places without the constraints of daily routines and schedules. But for us, those routines and schedules were a lifeline. Without them it felt as if we were drowning.

Patty took one boy to the cabin for a week to swim, join Junior Ranger activities at Big Trees State Park, and sleep outside in a two-person tent. Meanwhile, I stayed at home with the other child, where we had Treat Week. The boys were easy to be with when they were not together, and they prized the one-on-one attention. I fell in love with them again. We walked to the movies and rented videos; we stopped at Ben & Jerry's and got giant chocolate-dipped, sprinkle-covered waffle cones. Then Patty and I switched kids. Walking home from the library with me, Matt said, "I love Camp Mama and Camp Mommy."

At a cyber café near the university, Matt and a middle school friend joined other boys on Friday nights. Twenty computer screens were lit up with bloody battle video games with guns discharging, bombs exploding, aircraft crashing. But it was oddly silent for a gathering spot, oddly and wonderfully silent, because all the virtual warriors were wearing headphones. How I wished we could imitate that at home sometimes.

• • •

One summer, Matt and I spent ten days together when Spencer and Patty visited her parents in New Mexico. Our conflicts were brief and typical of a preadolescent and his mother. He did extra chores without fighting and helped me ready our bicycles for a ferry ride to Angel Island. He occasionally balked and started to argue, but it ended quickly. We went to Fosters Freeze for dessert; we rented seven movies; we rode bikes to and from his day camp. He was calm. Then Patty and Spencer returned home. Two hours later, Matt was having a fit over having to take a shower. The difference between being with only one parent for ten days and with the whole family for two hours was stunning.

Near the end of sixth grade, Matt asked us for green envelopes. "What do you need green envelopes for?" I asked him. He showed me a copy of a fake parking ticket his friends had passed around at school. "I want to put this on someone's car to scare them, to make them think they got a parking ticket. Wouldn't that be hecka funny?" It was harmless, I figured; it wasn't snapping off hood ornaments or taking a baby stroller off a front porch for a joyride down the hill and crashing it into the bushes, both of which middle schoolers had done on our street in the past, so I told him to call Office Depot for the envelopes. While he was on hold, Patty and I laughed. "Do you have Prince Albert in a can?" she whispered. When Matt got off the phone, we told him about the pranks that were popular when we were in junior high, long before caller ID. His favorite was the one I used: "Is your refrigerator running? Then you better go catch it." He got the joke, understood the double entendre, and laughed with us. I loved his naïveté.

• • •

Waikiki, where I'd found a cheap hotel room, smelled like flowering trees, sunscreen, and dryer softener sheets from hotels' housekeeping units. On Saturday, his twelfth birthday, I took Matt to a buffet breakfast at an open-air restaurant over-looking the beach. Because it was his birthday, I didn't urge him to try new foods or mandate vegetables, but let him eat whatever he wanted. He had eight pastries and six pieces of bacon. When I offered fruit, he chose a piece of watermelon, but pushed it aside when he found too many seeds in it.

Walking back to the hotel, he didn't anticipate or adjust to crowds. Instead, he bumped into me, knocking against my elbow again and again. He didn't understand the give and take, the subtle shifts, necessary to negotiate the sidewalk. I was beginning to understand that navigating the sidewalk was a just metaphor for his navigating the world.

I had known it was risky to take this kind of trip with him, pulling him away from home and his routines, making him sleep in a strange bed and tolerate a tropical heat he was not used to. I wanted him to have fun, to remember his twelfth birthday as a special time with his mom.

After breakfast, he flopped on his bed and channel-surfed. The TV made it impossible for me to read, so I left for a walk without him. He was inflexible in so many situations, I feared he'd never be able to live with someone or have a meaningful relationship, and thinking about that made me sad.

I wanted this trip so I could have some alone time with my boy. We reconnected when it was just the two of us, no little brother to complicate things, no parents disagreeing on how to discipline, no family drama. I wanted to commemorate his birth-day and also his passing into manhood. I didn't tell him this, of course, but I'd noticed the changes over the last few months. A pimple in the crease of his nose. Hairy man legs. My child-man wrapped a towel around his waist now after his shower. Earlier, when I'd asked the psychiatrist whether the increased tantrums could be due to the hormonal twitches of puberty, he'd said no, Matt was just getting older, stronger. I now believe he was wrong about this; I have heard so many parents complain of increased tantrums as their kids' bodies began to change. Hormones affect us in so many ways, we know now; they must uniquely affect kids with autism. The year before, when he was eleven, Matt was particularly short-tempered, like a preteen. One night when he was setting the table for dinner, Spencer was clicking his empty cap gun over and over. Before I could ask Spencer to stop, Matt did. When Spencer did not stop, Matt began banging a salad plate on the table until it broke. "Look what you did!" I shrieked. Matt looked up from the broken pieces. "Well, he was annoying me," he said, sounding perfectly justified.

My boy and I rented boogie boards at the beach in Honolulu and raced each other, shouting and squealing, to shore. We got lost on purpose in the steamy maze at the Dole plantation, and we snorkeled holding hands at Hanauma Bay Preserve. I insisted on a hike on Diamond Head, and although he complained every fifty feet about the heat and the distance, we made it to the top and took pictures of each other over-looking Waikiki. He loved pineapple ice cream and rainbows of shave ice, but the pizza he ordered for dinner had too much tomato sauce and he only ate half. He ordered a huge slice of cheesecake—without passion fruit sauce—and ate it all.

When he patted his full stomach after meals, I was irritated at his sloth. I worried that the combination of his starchy diet and lack of exercise would make him fat. He

wanted to watch TV, something we didn't do at home, and I
had to force him out of the room every day.

On our second morning, I packed the beach bags: towels,
fins and snorkels, lunch, sunscreen, and maps, and asked him
to get out his swim trunks. We'd been up since 5:00, our sleep
cycles rooted on the mainland.

"You do it," he said. "I'm busy."

This awakened my resentment, which quickly turned to
annoyance. "You're acting like a spoiled brat, like you're
helpless, like a handicapped person." I had the beach bag over
a shoulder, and I whisper-yelled at him through clenched teeth
so our neighbors wouldn't hear.

Recently, back at home, his little brother had begun offering to help me. He enjoyed pleasing me, relished in my praise.
When he and I visited Midwest relatives for spring break, he
told me, "I like traveling with you because you're organized,"
making me laugh. But I had to beg my eldest to help; he complained about most of my requests. It was as if he went from
toddler to teenager, skipping the stage where one gets pleasure
from pleasing their parents.

"I feel like I'm traveling with a two-year-old," I said. "I
have to do everything for you, and you do so little for me."

"You're a pumper knuckle," he said, and I couldn't tell if
he was trying to be funny.

But I was not in the mood. "Please don't call me names."

"You are too particular. Too fussy."

Jet lag had made me extra vulnerable, and I started to tear
up. "You say things that really hurt me."

He returned his gaze to the TV. "Can I call you a giraffe?"
he asked. "That's not an insult."

I ignored this.

"You are a flubberball," he said, poking my trapezius

muscle, finding a slight wiggle. "Blubber," he said, and I gave him a wounded look, because he needed to learn what was inappropriate, hurtful.

"Blubber. Flubber," he said.

In the rental car, on the way back from our trip to a northern beach, he was bored. He hummed, repeated phrases —repetitive noise, I labeled it—and when I said "shhh," he imitated that over and over.

"'Shhh' means be quiet," I said three times, aware of my own repetition.

Finally, in the confines of the rental car, I yelled. "Just shut your mouth. I just want to get away from you. This is why Jeremy doesn't want to be friends anymore, because you bug, bug, bug, and don't stop." I regretted saying this, and I didn't regret it. It simply felt good to get it out. I couldn't tell if it hurt him or if he believed me because his expression offered no clues.

The pool hushed him. He swam briefly, then sat in the hot tub and watched the teenagers play, swim, and smooch. I joined him for a while, and then retreated to a lounge chair to read.

With his disposable camera he captured images of breakfast buffets, stretch Hummer limousines, and our mango colored rental car. He didn't take pictures of me because I was right here with him. He was a boy in the present; I was already living in our future looking back on this moment. This trip was more marking a passage for me than it was for him.

I bought him a Jamba Juice for his birthday dinner, I picked up some sushi, and we ate at the beach as the sun slipped into the sea, silhouetted palm trees in the foreground just like on postcards. I surprised him with a visit to an arcade I'd found on an earlier solo walk, and he played games while I watched. When he used up all of the money I'd given him, he traded his tickets for M&Ms in a tube with a Bugs Bunny figure on top. When he pressed a button, Bugs Bunny, held up with skeletal strings, collapsed into a floppy muddle. I had the strange sense of knowing what this felt like.

We walked back to our hotel taking turns collapsing Bugs and laughing at the absurdity. Despite the evening crowds on the sidewalk, he did not bump into me the whole way. I sensed something had shifted in him, settled in place. In the room, he watched TV with the sound turned low, and I read about the fictional hostages in *Bel Canto*. For a moment, we were at peace.

And then it was time to go home.

10

The Toll

PATTY AND I WATCHED A MOVIE IN WHICH A MARRIAGE disintegrates once children are born. The stressed-out couple doesn't communicate, they argue about sharing the housework and childcare. I thought we were doing pretty well so far. Sure, it had been tough caring for a toddler and a baby, but we were a good team. We both changed diapers and vacuumed, alternated cooking and washing dishes, and we both earned paychecks. I was more worried about homophobia and protecting our kids from bigots than I was about my marriage dying. In the early 1990s, Patty and I had begun to come out at work. By telling the truth about our relationship, I hoped to get past the fear and shame. But mostly we were hunkered down in our house with our boys, our family.

After another of his tantrums when he was about ten, Matt found Patty and me in the kitchen, both dabbing at tears with tissues. Matt looked at us and asked Patty, "Why are you and Mommy sad?" She and I exchanged a glance, shook our heads. Matt definitely felt feelings, sometimes stronger than what appeared to fit the situation, especially frustration, which quickly turned to anger. And he could label many feelings; children whose parents are a teacher and psychologist are pretty much guaranteed to develop a strong feeling vocabulary. But at the time, we were frustrated by what looked like his selfishness. Matt didn't seem to care about others' feelings. He had plenty of empathy for animals in movies, though, crying openly when they died. When we rented the video *Born Free*, he asked through tears whether the orphaned lion cubs' "Mommy and Mama died." We couldn't put our fingers on it, though, and we didn't yet know about watching for his ability to take others' perspectives, much less to teach him this skill directly.

During Tantrum #476,000, I checked on Spencer in his room where he usually retreated to take cover when Matt blew. I rubbed Spencer's warm back with my palm, reminded him to use his headset to listen to music, breathe deeply, and think about his birthday party, and that we'd be up to talk with him, spring him from his room when the tantrum was over. The tantrum. What an inadequate word to describe this maelstrom of anger. It must have sounded like a murder in progress to Spencer listening from upstairs. I was beginning to grieve for his childhood, which was becoming marred by our inability to figure out why Matt behaved this way, much less what to do about it.

Downstairs, I rejoined Patty and Matt. I should have stayed out of it, let Patty handle it. But when I heard objects fly and Patty shrieking, I let myself get sucked back in. Every time.

"Go to your room now," I said, "and there won't be any other consequence. Just go."

But he stayed, following us when we walked away, unable to disengage. Stuck.

I started counting. "Matt, you have a one. Go to your room."

"That's not going to work," Patty said, shouting to be heard over his droning.

"Do you have an idea, Patty? Just jump in here anytime you have an idea!"

She looked wounded. "No, I just—"

"I know this isn't working, but at least I'm trying. Why don't you come up with something?"

"I don't have any ideas."

"Then don't criticize mine!" I shouted.

We were all stuck.

I cut out a *Peanuts* comic from the paper and stuck it on the wall near my computer. Psychiatrist Lucy asks Charlie Brown if his emotions feel like a roller coaster, and he says they feel more like bumper cars. Sometimes I felt like I was on both—a roller coaster with its climbs, thrills, falls, but then I was in those bumper cars, a free-for-all with the four of us crashing into each other and bouncing away, connected by a sparking electric charge under the same roof.

While the national divorce rate was around 50 percent, the divorce rate for partners raising children on the autism spectrum was around 80 percent. When I found this statistic in the newspaper when our kids were in high school, I was not surprised.

A friend of Spencer's came over, and on our front steps, I chatted with his mother for a while. I'd promised fourteen-year-old Matt a trip to the store, and he started doing his little routine to remind me. "Chop-chop. Come on. Vámanos!" I put up my hand in the stop signal and continued talking to the other mom. "Vámanos!" he said again. "Don't interrupt me," I said. He stood back for a couple of minutes, and then clapped his hands loudly three times. I ignored him. "Did he just clap at you?" the mother asked. "In my house," she said, "That would be cause for time in someone's room."

I wanted to push her down the steps.

When Matt was in middle school, the father of his best friend called one winter day. Matt and his son Sam had been inseparable in fifth grade. Patty had taken them both to our cabin for a few days back in August, and the boys hung out at the little lake paddling our blow-up boat, swimming, and fishing. Sam said it was the best vacation of his life.

"I miss seeing Matt," Sam's father said on the phone. And I realized we hadn't seen much of Sam lately, but that Matt had become close to another boy in his class recently. I figured it was just a shifting in friendships.

"I just wanted to tell you what happened, so you can help Matt if you want to."

"Of course," I said. Although I was sitting next to the heater, I shivered. What could have happened?

"Sam told me he doesn't want to be friends with Matt anymore."

"Oh, really?" My throat ached. "Did he say why?"

"Yeah, I asked him. Because Matt's my favorite of all his friends; I really enjoy him."

His kindness broke through my shell, and I felt I was about to be jabbed with a stick in an unprotected spot.

"But Sam said Matt does things that irritate him, and when he asks him to stop, he doesn't."

"Can you tell me what he did? So I can talk to Matt about it?" I struggled to keep my voice neutral, but it squeaked like a little girl's.

"Well, lemme see. Sam said that Matt poked him a bunch of times in class and wouldn't stop. He doesn't seem to realize when his friends say 'no' they mean it, they're not joking."

"Yeah, I know. Matt has a hard time with that." I tried to force the ball of pain from my throat. "Thanks for telling me this. I appreciate it."

"I figured you'd want to know, so you can help him with it."

"I miss Sam, too. He was my favorite of Matt's friends."

"Yeah, they were a good pair, weren't they?"

When we hung up, I didn't move from the chair for a long time.

Patty and I had no dinner parties, no barbecues, no coffee dates. We didn't get pizza with other families. We were hiding out, I see now, waiting for the tempests to pass, hoping we'd rejoin the social world again like we did when the kids were babies and toddlers. I'd felt less alone when we were trailblazer lesbian moms. We had support groups and potlucks and pool parties with other gay parents. But now, with a kid we hadn't quite figured out, and our family desperate to find its way, we hunkered down in our cave, just trying to survive. It was an insidious descent into isolation, one we were not even aware of. Not until many years had passed would we see how deeply we'd fallen into self-imposed seclusion. And not until many years had passed would we start to climb back out.

•   •   •

Although he wrote love notes when he was learning how to write, Matt did not usually say the words "I love you." When he was five, Spencer climbed into bed with me on a Saturday morning and watched me write in a journal. He held my elbow, breathing on my forearm while he studied my face. "Mommy, you write and you read; that's what you do. I love you; that's what I do." When I asked Matt once why he didn't tell us he loves us he said, "I already did." Even today, when I tell him I love him over the phone, he's silent or he simply says, "Okay." I guess those old love notes will have to last me a long time.

One Sunday, seven-year-old Matt found me on the couch writing in my journal. He lay down with me for two whole minutes, then sighed loudly and returned to his room to work on his homework. As I look through those journals now, I realize that I used them as therapy when times were scary and sad. I logged tantrums and explored grief while giving short shrift to the happy times. I didn't need them when we were a regular family enjoying trips to New Mexico, Hawaii, and Southern California or during the periods of calm at home. They were what I held onto when it felt like I was losing my mind.

I enjoyed the boys more when Patty was away visiting her parents, and it scared me that I was happier when the four of us were not together. It was easier being the only one in charge; the energy was different, more positive, less stressed. When the four of us were together, the anxiety infected us, voices got louder and more urgent. There was the scent of fear in the air, something toxic trickling in.

I see this now as typical of families in general; however, our family stress was exacerbated by Matt's trouble dealing with the added sensory input, inconsistency in parenting styles, and less predictability. When one parent was alone with the boys, the boys had a better sense of what was expected. And they couldn't do what most all kids do to their parents: divide and conquer.

Patty felt, too, that it was easier for her when I was out of town for a few days; the kids would get used to her style, and she'd become stronger in setting limits. However, almost every time I went away, I got a message from Spencer, in tears, telling me about Matt's latest scary outburst. Then I'd come home and take over again; it was our futile loop.

Our twentieth anniversary. The traditional gift is china, the modern one, platinum. In the past, I'd given Patty power tools, and she'd given me rosebushes for the garden. That year, though, we didn't exchange china, platinum, power tools, or flowers. Somehow we both knew it was the year to give each other just a card. Not cards reaffirming our vows, but cards that came from a feeling of obligation. "I don't need anything," we told each other. But it was a lie. We needed each other terribly, and we had nothing left to give.

I feared we would not make one more anniversary. We wanted to raise our kids, now fourteen and twelve, together, and I feared that splitting up would unbalance Matt, ruin his sense of consistency. I worried that it would make Spencer deeply and irreparably sad. But maybe our staying together was doing that. Do we stay together for the kids or split up for the kids? We were living the cliché.

• • •

One Sunday morning in early spring, when Patty and I were sharing the *San Francisco Chronicle* on the front steps and enjoying the warm sun and quiet, Spencer ran home from the park where he and Matt had taken our dog, Ruthie. When he reached our steps, the tears came.

"What's wrong?" Patty asked.

"He hit me on the back! Again and again. With Ruthie's ball chucker. 'You will do what I tell you!' he said. He bossed me and bossed me and bossed me even when I told him to stop it. So I ran home." Spencer was weeping, and the back of his shirt was splattered with mud from the swampy park. When he lifted his shirt to show us, small abrasions and a couple of bruises were already forming.

Then Ruthie, unleashed, arrived home, panting, her harness still across her snout. "He ordered me to pick up her leash, but he started hitting me, so I ran home. To get away from him."

I took him on my lap in the porch chair, careful not to touch his raw back. "You did the right thing."

Matt appeared, face flushed and wild. "Spencer left the leash at the park," he said, indignant. "I told him to bring it back, but he refused. He needs to go back and get it."

For the first time I saw my eleven-year-old son as a monster. He was hateful, violent, and losing touch with reality. He didn't see how he had hurt his brother. Worse, he didn't seem to care.

"Go get the leash, Matt," I said.

"No! Spencer is supposed to get it. That was his job."

"You hurt him. You go get it."

"NO!" he shouted, passing us and opening the screen door.

"Then get in your room. You're grounded for a week."

"No, I'm not. And I'm not going to my room."

"Yes, you are."

"No," he said. "I'm not!"

"Then you're grounded for two weeks."

He hung on the screen door, opening and closing it roughly.

"Get in your room," I said. "You're grounded."

He threw the hard plastic tennis ball chucker onto the front porch, and it bounced next to my foot. I nudged Spencer off my lap and toward the sidewalk. I wanted him far way from this disaster.

"I don't give a fuck!" Matt shouted.

"That'll be a dollar." For a time, we fined the boys for swearing.

"So what? I don't give a fuck!"

In a rare moment of clarity, I realized I didn't need to tell him he now owed two dollars; it could wait for later, he just needed to get into his room to calm down. Maybe if he calmed down we could avoid the tantrum.

But he didn't go, and instead somehow he was back outside, had passed me on the top step and Patty on the landing and was heading for Spencer. It was too late for me to catch him, and I didn't know what was going to happen and it happened too fast, but he was pounding with both fists on Spencer's back over and over until Patty finally wedged herself between them. Spencer screamed and then sobbed, and Matt stomped back into the house.

Patty and I went to Spencer. But I couldn't stand still, I was shaking so hard, and I couldn't believe the depth of my anger. I wanted Matt gone; I wanted him away from me, from Patty, from his brother, from the dog. I turned and faced Matt, now back outside standing on the top porch step. He was magnetically attracted to us, to continuing this battle. I pointed toward the house.

"Get in the house. Get in your room. You're grounded for a month!' Looking back, I know this was wrong, it was an unnecessarily long punishment, but when I said it, it didn't feel like enough. He had just beaten on his little brother, and that was not acceptable. I didn't stop to think that probably many brothers beat up on each other, but to me it was reprehensible. What was next? Drawing blood? Breaking a bone? Matt was at least a foot taller than his brother and outweighed him by forty pounds. I believed it was not enough of a punishment because he had clearly crossed a line; he was out of control. He had been beating on him for a deranged reason: Spencer wouldn't pick up the dog's leash.

I followed Matt into the house; he and I met in the front hall next to the brass hooks that held sweatshirts and jackets and the shoes we lined up on a low shelf. When I spoke to him I did not look into his eyes, but to the side of his face. I was trying to thwart this tantrum with a method I'd learned at the animal shelter. Don't approach the dog face-to-face since that can be seen as threatening. Rather, turn sideways, drop eye contact.

But he refused to go into his room. He shouted in my face and I recoiled. How dare he shout at me? Children should not be allowed to do this. I raised my hand and moved to slap his face. I wanted to feel his cheek on my palm. I wanted to snap him out of it; I wanted to punish him.

But I missed, got only air, and he approached me, pounding with his fists on my forearms; and this was when I knew we were both out of control, that I would not try to slap him ever again. But I needed to make him stop. I yelled. I backed up next to the hooks. He shouted again, and this part remains fuzzy because I was so angry, my body was trying to flee, but I was also trying to show him who was boss. I was angry that he had hit me, kicked my shin and my slippered foot.

Finally, I moved to the phone and started dialing. "I'm calling the police," I said. "Get in your room." He turned and went to his room. I hung up before I finished dialing, fell into the chair, put my face in my hands, and sobbed.

The next morning, a neighbor asked why I was limping. "Stubbed my toe," I lied. My fourth toe was puffy, bruised at the place it met the foot, purple sunset colors underneath the tender folds. The skin on top, near the tiny nail, was stretched so tight it burned, like it was about to pop open, letting the blood, which was collecting underneath, spurt out. On the phone with the doctor's office, I came closer to the truth. "I got kicked." To the nurse practitioner I said, "I got in the way of my son's foot. It was an accident."

11

D i a g n o s i s

---

au·tism [**aw-tiz-*uh*m**] *n.*

1. a pervasive developmental disorder of children, characterized by impaired communication and socialization, excessive rigidity, and emotional detachment.

2. a tendency to view life in terms of one's own needs and desires.

I WANTED TO TAKE OFF MY SHOE AND SOCK AND SHOW DR. A., the psychiatrist, my broken toe. It was still purple and brown and buddy taped to the toe next to it; it still throbbed when I stepped on it a certain way. I wanted to show him the bruises I hadn't found until a few days after Matt's tantrum, bruises on my forearms and the one on the first joint of my left index finger, defense wounds maybe, some still tender to the touch. It was like the aftermath of a car accident, when the victim discovers hidden injuries she didn't know she'd suffered because the adrenaline had protected her from feeling the initial blows.

At home, I had shown eleven-year-old Matt my broken toe, my bruises. I'd forced him to look at the bruises in the middle of Spencer's back and on his skinny chicken-wing shoulder blade, bruises I'd discovered when Spencer practiced piano shirtless one evening. One of the bruises looked like a punctuation mark, a giant colon, and I wondered if it had been the tennis ball chucker or Matt's knuckles that had made that odd mark. "Are you sorry you did this?" I'd asked Matt, forcing him to look at Spencer's back. "Yes," he said after a pause that made me doubt his remorse. He had learned what he was supposed to say. It was what his fourth grade teacher had said two years earlier, "He doesn't seem to feel remorse." I was just now starting to see it.

In Dr. A's office in Berkeley, I introduced my son. "This is a wonderful boy," I said to the short, smooth-faced man with straight blond hair covering the tops of his ears. He looked no more than twenty, but diplomas from Stanford and the University of California hung on the wall behind him, and I wondered whether he had children, whether he knew what he was doing, whether he would help us. I was aware we were about to spend the good part of an hour talking about Matt's behavior problems in front of him, and that there wouldn't be time for listing all of his positive qualities, the attributes that still made him my joy boy. "He's smart, he's a whiz at math, he's good at sharing," I smiled at Matt. "Well, most of the time."

Matt was picking at his nails and looked stricken, as if he was about to be carted off to jail.

"And he's honest," I said, laughing.

Dr. A's smile looked forced. "I'm sure he is a wonderful boy," he said with a bumpy accent that I guessed was French. He was building rapport with us; I'd learned how to do that in my training program, too. "So why have you come to see me?"

Patty and I described the most recent tantrum, and then Dr. A. guided us in a lengthy history taking, for which he made no notes. In my work when I interview parents, I take copious notes because I have to write lengthy reports, and background information is expected. Plus, in some instances now, I'm the first to recognize the signs of an autism spectrum disorder, and I need to lay it all out, like an attorney arguing a case. Also, in order to get kids special education services, I have to show how the student meets the eligibility criteria. And probably, since I'm a public school psychologist providing a free service, I feel a need to prove that I know what I'm doing. At times, I'm envious of physicians who can rubber-stamp patients with a diagnosis without the hours of testing, report writing, and meetings.

Listening to Dr. A. that day in 2004, I recognized many of the questions designed to sift out a diagnosis.

Are there any repetitive motions, any hand-flapping? No. *He doesn't have autism.*

Does he line up objects, count things excessively? No. *It's not OCD.*

Inability to focus? Lots of excess energy? No. *It's not ADHD.*

Limited interests? Lack of friends? No, he has a handful of friends, the brainy boys from elementary school. He's a little obsessed with the Giants, but aren't lots of boys? *I'm not sure what we're ruling out here.*

Lack of empathy? *No, he hugs me when I cry.*

Difficulties learning? No, he's a whiz at math, we say again. And he likes to read. *He doesn't have a learning disability.*

Dr. A. listened to our descriptions of Matt's development, his getting "stuck" on ideas and questions, his need for black-and-white answers to questions, his extreme frustration at the responses "maybe" and "I don't know," his raging when his

routine changed. The tantrums. How his best friend had
stopped calling this year.

He asked Matt, "Are you mostly happy, sad, or angry?" He
had to repeat it before Matt understood what he was asking;
his accent was confusing Matt. I was very interested in this
question. Was the doctor ruling out depression? I saw my boy
as mostly happy, then angry, and then sad, in that order. But
how did he see himself? Without looking at me, which he so
often did when he didn't know what to say, Matt said,
"Happy." I let out the air I had been sucking in.

Finally, the doctor had heard enough, and he sent Matt to
the waiting room. "Let me get right to it,' he said. "First of
all," he directed to me. "You are a psychologist, right?"

"Yes."

"Ph.D.?"

"Yes." I shot a look at Patty. "Patty is his other mother," I
said.

"I taught special education for thirty-three years," she said.

He glanced at Patty and then spoke to me again. "What
do *you* think it is?"

I shrugged. "I think it's sensory integration disorder with
emotional dysregulation." But for the first time my voice was
full of doubt. I no longer knew what I believed.

"Let me tell you what *I* think it is," he said. "I think your
son has borderline to mild Asperger's syndrome."

Patty and I locked eyes for a second. She looked impressed, but I knew she was as clueless as I was. I'd had some
trouble understanding the psychiatrist's accent over the
telephone and during the interview. He had spoken quickly
and I could not decipher a few words until he repeated them.
But his last sentence was perfectly clear, and I would never
forget it. It had never occurred to me that my son might be

showing signs of Asperger's, and this lack of understanding even what Asperger's syndrome was suddenly made me ashamed.

It was 2004, way before Asperger's had found its way into the popular media, and I had a fuzzy recollection of a seminar about Asperger's that I'd attended at work a couple of years earlier. I wondered if I still had the notes I'd taken. I could picture the large room where the forty-some of us school psychologists had met that day, but no matter how hard I tried, I couldn't remember what we'd learned. At that point in my career, I had never identified a student with Asperger's. It was one of those rare diagnoses, like bipolar disorder—still known as manic depression then—and I just didn't have experience with it. At the time, I believed I'd never assessed a student with Asperger's. Now, of course, I know I had, but I hadn't known what I was seeing.

I rubbed the hard plastic arm of the chair. "I never thought of that."

"I see at least one autistic child or adolescent every day. Sometimes two or three." He was smiling again, as if proud of his experience, his diagnostic acumen.

But I didn't understand why he was telling us about autistic patients. I was sure he saw patients with many kinds of conditions, but what did autism have to do with Matt?

Autistic meant the kids I'd worked with in San Francisco when I first moved to California, the kids who flapped their hands and echoed what I said to them. Autism is an either/or. You are autistic or you're not. Even while I was thinking this, I knew I was wrong. I'd read about the autism spectrum; I knew there were milder forms. I knew that the number of people diagnosed with Asperger's had been rising, but when I thought of Asperger's, I thought of the newspaper articles I'd read about Silicon Valley, where computer programmers' children were being diagnosed with Asperger's at an astounding rate, and then some of the parents realized their own quirkiness fit the Asperger's profile. But this shouldn't have been happening to the son of a teacher and a school psychologist.

The rest of the appointment began to blur. Dr. A. wanted Matt to try Risperdal, the anti-psychotic that Patty's ninety-year-old father took for late-in-life onset hallucinations. Risperdal was not FDA approved for children. The autism spectrum. My son was on the autism spectrum. Borderline to mild Asperger's. He was barely on the autism spectrum, I needed to believe. AUTISTIC sounded too serious, like CANCER. Way too scary.

On the drive home from Dr. A's office, the three of us were quiet. We told Matt about the prescription, that there might be a medicine to help with the tantrums, and then we were silent. I ruminated. Why us? What caused it? Maybe the sperm donor didn't tell the truth in his medical history. But twelve years earlier, when I'd been pregnant with Matt, most people had never heard of Asperger's.

I needed to run to a book to refresh my memory about Asperger's. I'd known only a couple of children diagnosed with Asperger's, like the fifth grader the previous year who at recess walked on tiptoes pacing the perimeter of the school yard, running his fingers over the chain link fence. I remembered his obsession with Harry Potter, his mother's tears at meetings. But it was usually speech and language therapists who worked with kids with Asperger's in the public schools. I didn't remember studying Asperger's in grad school back in the early eighties; it wasn't added to the *DSM-IV* until 1994,

when Matt was a year old. And the children I remembered
from the playground were much more impaired than Matt. I
wondered if Dr. A. could be wrong.

Perhaps something had happened when I was pregnant to
cause Matt's sensory quirks and tantrums. We'd always teased
him that he didn't get cold because his nerve endings didn't
reach his skin; what if the dendrites in his brain hadn't
migrated their entire route, but had been blocked by something? I didn't smoke or drink when I was pregnant, but I had
used the microwave. And I worked in an elementary school
that was later remodeled, asbestos and who knows what else
removed. In the seventh month of my pregnancy, our dog,
Mimi, died. I had grieved physically for her. Did that
emotional trauma cause it? My psychologist voice said *You're
being ridiculous*. My mother voice was louder, asking *What did you
do wrong?*

After we dropped Matt back at school, Patty took the
prescription to the drug store and I logged on to the Internet
to read about Risperdal's side effects. Alopecia, bullous erup-
tion, furunculosis, hypertrichosis, urticaria, genital pruritus. I
had to look up all the words in a medical dictionary. Hair loss,
blisters, boils, hair growth, hives, genital itching. It all sounded
ghastly, but at least it wasn't "trouble breathing."

I didn't want to give the medicine to him, but I thought
about the tantrums, my purple toe, the smashed mirror, the
broken picture glass, Spencer's bruises.

I emailed two friends about the diagnosis, using the words:
weird, in shock, disturbing, freaking out. It was easier to write
it than say it. I wanted both the instant connection of email
and the safety of hiding behind it. If I'd picked up the phone
or told someone in person, I wouldn't have been able to get
the words past my choked-up throat. But I didn't know how to

spell the stupid syndrome. Was it burger? I looked it up. Ass? No, it was asp, like a snake.

I didn't tell my writing group, whose meeting I had missed because of the appointment with the psychiatrist.

I didn't tell my neighbor, whose two-year-old had been showing signs of a sensory disturbance recently, balking at clothing tags, socks, long-sleeved shirts, and long pants.

I didn't tell my mother, to whom I had just given a book on sensory integration disorder. I could have said, yes, I'll pick you up from the airport, and let's go to the symphony this month, and, by the way, your grandson has Asperger's. That's why he drives us crazy, that's why it's harder to be around him than your other grandson.

I didn't tell people yet. I was ashamed, scared. I didn't know what to say.

That afternoon, before the kids got home from school, I ran to Cody's bookstore and pulled books about Asperger's off the shelves. I read half of one sitting on the cement floor at the store, and within two minutes I knew that Dr. A. was right. Each page held an affirmation.

Extreme reactions (tantrums) to minor upsets.

Difficulty being flexible, changing plans. Gets stuck on topics.

Upset by ambiguous language. Interprets language literally.

Concrete and literal thinker. Prefers things to be black and white.

Difficulty making and keeping friends.

Poor fine motor and/or gross motor coordination.

I bought the book and at home stuck Post-its on the pages I wanted to copy for his sixth grade teachers. Getting busy kept me from weeping.

We had the right name for it now, and knowing that initially brought a sense of relief. There were professionals who could help; there were lists in the back of the book. We would ask his school for help. We could shift some of the responsibility, the burden, over to Dr. A. He would take care of us. But a second later, I was back to wondering. Was it genetic? Did it run in *my* family? Some of us were quirky, some of us were particular about neatness and order.

That night, I dreamed I was at the foot of a hill, walking in the street. I took a step up the hill, and it felt like I was moving through sludge. My body was so heavy I took two steps and was overcome with dizziness. I sat on the ground in the street. Patty appeared, and I told her, "I can't get up the hill."

When I woke up the next morning, my first thought was that it was only a dream, the Asperger's was just a dream. It was still just the old familiar sensory integration dysfunction.

That morning before work, I found on the website of a woman whose father, brother, and two sons had Asperger's a long list of the positive qualities of "Aspies" described in a cloying, Pollyanna tone. I was shocked by her enthusiasm, her cheerleading for Asperger's. Patty and I did not yet completely appreciate the strengths related to Asperger's. Aspects like honesty, persistence at certain tasks, strong memory, attention to details, work ethic, and novel problem-solving methods. We did appreciate Matt's honesty—and inability to lie—as well as his ease with entertaining himself when alone, even though at times he would complain of boredom and seem desperate to play with Spencer or play computer games to fill empty spaces in his day.

"You should be a lawyer," we'd told Matt a few times. He could argue against us until we wanted to bang our heads against a wall. Reading the woman's website, I was not in the cheerleading frame of mind. Mostly, I still wanted to play on the team that would trounce the Asperger's. At that point, I thought of it as a disease, one that could be cured. I wanted to fix him, as if he was broken. It would be years of reading and working with scores of students that would teach me a different way to think about it.

That afternoon, I met Spencer after school, and as we walked home I was more distracted than ever. I wanted to ask him: *Do you know your brother has Asperger's? That's why he acts the way he does. I'm sorry, but you'll have to deal with this shit your whole life.*

On the way home, feeling a rising sense of irritation, I wanted to shout to the neighbors, "My son has Asperger's!" Except sometimes I confused the word with Alzheimer's. Asperger's didn't exactly roll off my tongue yet. I turned and stared at Spencer walking next to me. He seemed so normal, so unbelievably typical, everything you'd expect of a nine-year-old boy. He had not changed, but now with his brother's diagnosis, he seemed even more "regular." It was like when he was born, and twenty-three-month-old Matt suddenly looked huge next to his newborn brother. Even though Matt hadn't changed overnight, something else had. Our perception.

As I read more about Asperger's, I realized it was not going to go away. Matt might have been growing out of the sensory integration disorder—he had become less tactilely defensive—but the Asperger's would not simply disappear. From the books I'd skimmed in the store, I knew we'd have to learn new ways to deal with him, and he'd have to be taught directly the skills he'd need to make and keep friends, to understand body language and facial expressions and sarcasm. But he would always have Asperger's, and we would always be teaching him. And at that time, I had no idea how much he would teach me and how I would use it in my work with other kids on the spectrum.

For a time, I hoped that having the diagnosis would relieve some of the conflict between Patty and me. Maybe it would give us a path to follow together.

But the diagnosis also brought pain. That night, I sat in my reading chair and wrote in my journal: *It feels as if someone has died. It's as if my boy, the boy I thought I would watch grow up, is gone. It's the death of the future I'd imagined, and the sadness sinks into my belly. It's been raining for days and all night last night. I need the sun now, or I'll disappear into a cloud.*

When I returned home from work the next day, Matt was sitting in the reading chair next to the picture window. He was holding a book with an apricot-colored cover that I recognized, *The Curious Incident of the Dog in the Night-Time.* I couldn't help but laugh out loud in disbelief at this choice of books, as it was a novel whose protagonist is a British teenager with Asperger's. We had not yet told him about the diagnosis; we were giving ourselves some time to understand it ourselves before we explained it to him. "Where did you get that book?" I practically screeched.

"Mrs. Moore gave it to me."

"Your math and science teacher? Why this book?"

"She's letting a bunch of us read it. It has a lot of math in it. Why are you asking me that?"

"No reason. It's a good book. I've got a copy on my shelf." I couldn't believe the irony, the synchronicity.

Matt lay on the floor at our feet with his long body stretching from one end of the couch to the other. At eleven years, he was five feet three inches. In the evenings recently, the boys and I had been watching their baby videos. When they were little, I'd picked up the video camera often. I'd wanted to capture their increasing vocabularies, their baby voices and baby play. I'd forgotten so much, like how Matt talked slowly and with a gravelly voice. He was a boy wearing sweatpants and long-sleeved shirts—which he would later give up in favor of shorts and Giants tee shirts—enthusiastically singing "Happy Birthday" and "Down by the Bay." In the videos, four-year-old Matt gave an Easter egg to his two-year-old brother because "Spencer doesn't have a yellow one yet."

Two weeks after we heard the diagnosis, Patty and I were ready to tell Matt. We had finally called and told our parents and our siblings. We wanted to make sure Matt understood he was not to blame, so Patty and I rehearsed what we wanted to say. If he remembered this moment for the rest of his life, we wanted him to remember that his parents had sat on either side of him on the couch and told him in just the right way, with so much love he would never forget it.

"Dr. A. told us what's causing the tantrums."

"What?" Matt looked at me, then at Patty sitting on his other side.

"It's called Asperger's and a lot of people have it and it's not your fault and now that we know what it is we can help you."

"Yeah, Uncle Dan already told me." His voice was composed. I believed he was more intrigued by the event, the rare family meeting on the couch, than by the subject, but since his face was void of expression, I didn't know for sure.

"What?" I said, my voice rising. I couldn't believe my brother had scooped us.

"Uncle Dan told me."

"He told you that you have Asperger's?"

"Yeah, or something that sounds like that."

I looked past him at Patty, resisting the urge to raise my eyebrows and shake my head and scream *what the hell!*

"Huh. He told you?"

"Is that okay?"

"I wanted Mama and me to tell you, but since you already know, I don't know. Do you have any questions?"

"No."

"No?"

"What should I ask you?"

"How dare he?" I whispered. Patty and I were hiding out in our breakfast room, the door to the rest of the house closed. "Why would he think it's all right to tell Matt when we haven't had a chance? We're the parents. It should have come from us. He had no right." My throat closed against the tears that were forming.

"I'm not defending him," Patty said, "but maybe he thought we already had. It took us a couple of weeks."

"He should have asked us."

"Yeah, he should have."

"I feel like he stole something from us." I let the tears come.

When I finally opened up the *DSM-IV* and found Asperger's, the word "disorder" made me wrinkle up my nose in repulsion. In the parenting books I'd read at the bookstore, it was called a syndrome, not a disorder. A syndrome is a collection of symptoms or behaviors; a disorder does not sound so benign, and it suggests an impairment or a disease.

When I looked up the word "disorder" recently, though, and read "lack of order or regular arrangement; confusion,"[35] I believed it was a perfect description of Asperger's. I have often felt that Matt's brain was out of order, and we were all

---

[35] *Webster's Unabridged Dictionary*, second edition. Random House, 2001.

most definitely confused! So many of the students I see now
are truly suffering and seem rather disordered, socially and
emotionally. And the synonyms for disorder were also fitting:
riot, turbulence, brawl, disturbance, uproar. Our family was
certainly in an uproar: a tumult, a bustle and clamor of many
voices, often because of a disturbance. Back then the term felt
insulting. But it all fits the 1000-piece puzzle now.

I wanted to blame the sperm donor's genes, but in some ways
Matt was like me. I got stuck. I could be inflexible. I still don't
like noise, especially in the morning. When a hairdresser drops
a clump of hair onto my forehead, I scrunch my nose and
blow it off. Sometimes jackets feel too heavy, too constricting.
Matt and I argued, both of us stubborn, locked into our
positions. I wanted him to obey me more than I wanted to give
in to him. "You need to be more flexible," Patty often told me.
"And you need to be more firm, more consistent," I replied. It
was our most basic conflict.

Grounding kept the boys apart after the leash and ball chucker
incident, and Matt read stacks of books when his other
privileges were taken away. After a week or two, though, we let
him earn time off for good behavior. He did all of his chores
without complaining. He was so eager to see his brother
during meals and rides in the car that it brought peace to the
house for a time, and although Matt complained that grounding wouldn't change his behavior in the future, Patty and I felt
it worked. We were rewarded with the quiet and were more
likely to use grounding again the next time. But raising Matt
cannot be compared to raising a neurotypical child. The

methods that work with those kids did not work with Matt because he was not able to understand what we were doing; it didn't make any sense to him, and he had strong arguments against it. Therapists tried to help us in a piecemeal fashion, but it wasn't enough. Now that I think about it, we, an educated parenting couple, probably needed a program like those for children with more severe autism: a daily, in-home behavioral and social training program. Training us parents to understand Matt's perspective and training Matt to make sense of ours. We needed to learn how to "hold" Matt metaphorically while teaching him how the world worked, and while we figured out how to guide him through it.

"I'm not taking any medicine!" Matt said when Patty set the Risperdal pill next to his cereal bowl.

"Why not?" Patty asked.

"I don't want to."

"We need you to try it, to see if it will help your body feel better."

"I don't want to."

"Are you afraid it will make you feel funny?"

"No."

"What is it then?"

"I don't like taking pills; I hate taking pills."

As a kid I'd crushed aspirin in applesauce to get it down. We offered Matt the tiny pill, cut in half, only a quarter of a milligram, with candy, with ice cream, with butter like Grandma's old cats took their pills. Finally, he agreed to rip off a piece of a PowerBar, chew it a minute, and then swallow the pill with it. We began to buy PowerBars in bulk.

But the medicine was no cure. He had two explosions in one day. I didn't think it possible that he could summon the energy to rise to another one. The second ended with Matt pounding on Patty's arms, me intervening again, and Patty calling the psychiatrist but not being able to speak after the woman at the answering service said, "What's the matter, hon?"—this touch of humanity completely breaking any remaining defenses Patty might have had. With tears running down her cheeks and dripping onto the kitchen floor, she handed me the phone, and when the doctor came on the line, I told him Matt was in his room smashing a baseball bat into the floor, and we were stopping the medicine. This one ended with Dr. A. advising us to call the police if he didn't stop. It ended with Patty and me canceling our dinner reservations, giving my mother, who had been planning on babysitting, our theater tickets. It ended with me crying at the kitchen counter and nine-year-old Spencer standing beside me rubbing my back. It ended with me telling Matt he had wrecked our evening, wrecked our whole day, and him retorting, "Well, you're wrecking my *life!*" It ended with me believing and not wanting to believe that I was wrecking his life. It ended with me weeping because the believing it was winning.

During one of the tantrums, he and I were at the top of the stairs, and he would not descend. He screamed, he beat his hands on his thighs, he took shallow breaths and let out erratic cries. Tears streamed down his face, landing on the hardwood floor next to his bare feet. I knew now that he could not help this, that he was stuck because of a screwed-up circuit in his brain that prevented him from understanding me.

1-2-3 Magic had lost its spell; we'd given it up. For a long time, I'd thought he was manipulating us, but now I understood he was doing this because he thought Patty or I would back down, that we would make it right, or at least what he believed was right. Even then I knew he was not doing this to anger me; he was not enjoying it, he was miserable. He was physically stuck, and this knowledge wrapped a protective bubble around him. At these times, I was able to stay disengaged. Even though I was yelling, demanding to be heard, to be the authority, I was not shouting from rage. I was annoyed, frustrated that what we were doing wasn't working; I was angry that he was not obeying, but there was a new feeling during this tantrum. Sympathy. I felt sorry for my boy when he was like this, crying, wiping his eyes with his palms. His voice was raw; his throat must have been burning.

I had an image of an old LP record stuck in one groove, a record skipping, unable to proceed to the next one. I had an impulse to flick the needle, do something to jolt Matt out of this groove. But I knew I could not. Both Patty and I had slapped him once before, I had clapped my hands loudly next to his ears. But, of course, those misguided attempts only infuriated him. For a person with normal sensory input, maybe some kind of surprise could jolt them out of the stuck place. But for a person with an extra-sensitive sensory system, the same thing must make them feel as if they were under attack, that they must protect themselves at all costs.

Just like a video card that didn't work in the boys' computer, I believed Matt's brain was not programmed correctly, or it was missing the software that took care of flexibility in thinking, socializing, and emotional regulation. So when he got stuck, when his face turned red, and he made me crazy by screaming "why?" I knew it was the Asperger's.

We had to help him learn how to get unstuck, but not by shocking or smacking him. He was so smart, maybe if we presented it logically, with no room for ambiguity—if such a thing was possible—maybe he'd comply. But we didn't know how to do that yet.

. . .

"Theory of mind *refers to the notion that many autistic individuals do not understand that other people have their own plans, thoughts, and points of view. Furthermore, it appears that they have difficulty understanding other people's beliefs, attitudes, and emotions.*

"*By not understanding that other people think differently than themselves, many autistic individuals may have problems relating socially and communicating to other people. That is, they may not be able to anticipate what others will say or do in various situations. In addition, they may have difficulty understanding that their peers or classmates even have thoughts and emotions, and may thus appear to be self-centered, eccentric, or uncaring.*

"*Interestingly, people with autism have difficulty comprehending when others don't know something. It is quite common, especially for those with savant abilities, to become upset when asking a question of a person to which the person does not know the answer.*"[36]

Reading this helped me. The next time I said, "I don't know," and Matt cried or yelled, "What do you mean, you don't know?" I would try to explain. I would try not to get angry with him. I would try to understand.

What Set Him Off

• Ambiguous or imprecise answers: "Maybe," "I don't know," and "We'll see."

---

[36] Stephen M. Edelson, Ph.D., Center for the Study of Autism, Salem, Oregon.

- Lies.
- A change in expectations.
- Not getting his way.
- Abrupt ending to a pleasurable activity.
- A burrito cut the wrong way.
- Broken rules.
- Something seen as unfair.
- An illogical argument.
- Not understanding intentions of others, idioms, body language, tone of voice, facial expressions.
- Being hungry. Being tired. Starting to get sick.

I was drained, depleted, tired of carrying loads of emotional laundry around. I wanted to sleep deeply. We were not doing well, our little Asperger's family in its tiny house. When we were all together for too long, we were all now in the steam cooker, and it seemed the pressure would blow off the roof. Patty and I were not parenting well together; ironically it felt as if there was nothing holding us together but the children. We talked about her moving out, me moving out, us rotating in and out of the house so the kids could stay in place. I went to bed earlier and earlier every night; it was my failure to cope. Spencer got up early every morning so he could get out of the house. He went to his middle school to hang out with his friends before the bell rang; it was his escape. If I felt this much stress and could barely handle it, I didn't know how an eleven-year-old could manage. Or how our family could survive.

12

———

B u s m a n ' s   H o l i d a y

busman's holiday *n.*

a vacation or day off from work spent in an activity closely resembling one's work, as a bus driver taking a long drive.

IN THE ELEMENTARY SCHOOL WHERE I WORKED FOR TEN years when the boys were young, I visited most of the classrooms to teach the students and the teachers conflict resolution methods that I'd cobbled together. I placed posters in classrooms and in the hallways outlining the steps and led children in relaxation methods. On the playground, I reminded kids to use the conflict resolution steps when they squabbled over kickballs and four square rules. I was the school's expert at conflict resolution. In the staff room at lunch, the teachers thanked me. "You must be such a good mom," someone said, and I felt like an imposter.

A fourteen-year-old boy drowned in a city pool during an eighth grade end-of-the-year trip one June. I was called out as part of a crisis team to talk to kids and consult with distraught staff. For two hours, I listened and comforted. I walked through the school's grief but didn't feel it. I was a professional at work. Then I got in my car to drive home and realized the boy was exactly the same age as Matt. I rested my forehead on the steering wheel and cried.

I was assigned an extra case—assessing a thirteen-year-old boy in a residential school for children with emotional disturbances. Despite his diagnosis of oppositional defiant disorder, he laughed at my jokes and cooperated with every task I gave him. At home, he threw glasses and smashed plates. Here, with me, he was an angel. My son was an angel in school, too. The irony threatened to shatter something fragile inside me.

"I feel like such a bad mother," I told Betsy, a therapist who had been treating children with sensory integration disorder since before it was known as sensory integration disorder. We saw her when Matt was ten, before we knew about Asperger's. Her office was a large room with a couch and chairs as well as a corner with a sand tray and shelves of miniatures. I'd used a sand tray with kids at work to help them show me what was worrying them. But then, in the therapist's office, I wanted to kneel next to the box, run my fingers through the miniature beach, and build a mandala out of shells and stones.

     "I feel like a failure," I said, sitting on the couch next to Patty. "About having no more patience, about losing my temper—I spanked him a few months ago; I feel horrible." I had to wait a moment before I could speak again. "It's just so hard to deal with him when he gets stuck. I know I shouldn't yell at him; it only intensifies the tantrum. And spanking him was the worst thing to do. It only made him furious, made him hate me. I'm a psychologist, for God's sake. I work with children. I'm supposed to know what to do."

She placed her notebook on the table and leaned forward. "It's harder for us, isn't it?" she said, and I let go a silent exhalation. "First, there are the challenges of raising a child with special needs, and add to that the expectations that we will always know what to do, that we should be able to get everything right." Her voice was melodious and hypnotic. I thought of a harbor horn guiding boats back to their berths, and I sank deeper into the couch. Finally, someone understood what I was going through. It sounded as if she may have had a similar situation. "And then, of course, there are the expectations we put on ourselves. Those can be pretty high, can't they?"

My tears then were those of relief. She had seen right into me, had born witness to our secrets, and for the first time in months, if not years, I felt hope again. Hope that we would survive Matt's childhood.

At Fred Volkmar's[37] Asperger's presentation in the fall of 2005, I didn't yet recognize the irony of the busman's holiday—that I was attending a professional conference wearing the hats of both a psychologist and a mother, that I was on a long busman's holiday, never really getting a vacation from Asperger's. At the time, I simply anticipated the professional training to keep myself current, or rather to catch up with this area in which I'd lagged behind.

Before beginning, Volkmar cautioned the group of several hundred that the film clips of children with Asperger's might

---

[37] Psychologist and researcher at the Yale Child Study Center.

make them laugh, but that the clips might also make the parents in the audience sad. My eyes immediately filled with tears, and I tossed away my professional hat. I was a mother, there for self-preservation and taking care of my family. During the conference, I had to remind myself to take notes so I could apply what I was learning to the kids I was assessing at work and share what I'd learned with my colleagues. But it was almost impossible. I was a mother first.

A few years ago, I tested a nonverbal boy with autism and gave him a Goldfish cracker every time he did what I asked him to. But when I came to get him from his classroom the second time, he was working on a worksheet, and he cried and screamed and hopped in place. "I'll come back after math time," I said.

Another year, I evaluated two six-year-old boys with autism, one after the other. One was so severely affected—he wore a diaper, ate with his fingers, and mouthed a squeaky baby toy that he occasionally tapped with rigidly bent fingers —he didn't look even when I held Goldfish crackers or a piece of candy in front of him.

The other boy recognized numbers and letters and was learning to read. He repeated what people said to him, including my "That's not okay" when he grabbed at the crackers. You never realize what phrases you use over and over until a kid with autism starts repeating you. He tipped his chair back and looked at me for a reaction—social engagement, I noted. But on the playground, he knelt on the spongy rubber under the play structure and dug in the cracks for stones.

I was still awed at the range of possibilities, the relative placement on the spectrum of autistic-ness. A roll of the genetic dice.

• • •

At work, I asked a mother what she thought was going on with
her four-year-old son, a boy who looked at no one, spun books,
and rocked forward and back like he was on a rocking horse.
"I wonder if he's artistic," she said, using the wrong word. "I
have a cousin who's artistic." I understood that it was probably
a regional way of speaking, like an accent, that made her use
the more common word. This mother was not highly educated; she may not have paid close attention to the word
autistic before. I tried not to overemphasize my pronunciation.

"Kids with autism have problems in three areas," I said,
launching into my brief lesson about the impairments in
communication, socialization, and behavior. I gave her examples
of her son's behavior and how it fit with an autism diagnosis.
"Autism," I said, "is genetic; it runs in families, mostly in the
men. People are born with it, and it's nobody's fault." These
were the most important facts I could give, I believed, and she
nodded as if relieved but not totally believing me yet. When I
was done, she stood to leave. She reached out her hand to
shake mine. "Thank you," she said, holding my hand a beat
longer than usual. "I pretty much knew he was artistic."

A few days later, I sat with another mother in my office
and told her what Dr. A. first told me. Your son has Asperger's.
I was surprised by the tears of empathy that I had to blink
back. I explained that her eight-year-old's difficulties making
friends, not understanding facial expressions, his narrow and
deep interest in animal taxonomy, and his demand to know what
to expect were all part of the syndrome. She nodded solemnly,
and when I finished, she stared at her shoes. "I knew something wasn't right," she said. "But the doctor said he was fine."

I remembered the kids I worked with at the Saturday

recreation program in San Francisco. How autism then meant body rocking and twirling, no eye contact, echolalia, tantrums, virtually no communication or social interaction. Most of the kids I worked with back then went to state hospitals when they got too big for their parents to handle.

Now, more than twenty years later, autism was described as a cluster of behaviors ranging across a spectrum, a continuum on which we place children and adults based on the severity of their difficulties with socialization, communication, and repetitive or stereotypical behaviors. I pictured it as a horizontal line ranging from those who are simply quirky, to those who behave oddly but could also "pass," to those with the most severe autistic characteristics. I imagined it as a long line because no two individuals hold the same spot, and placement along the continuum would be flexible because people move along it as they learn new skills and mature. The *DSM-5*[38] is more in line with this simpler way of conceptualizing autism; it now has three levels: mild, moderate, and severe.

I'm ambivalent over the dropping of Asperger's from the *DSM-5*. As a mother, I'm somewhat protective of the label because it's now part of Matt's identity, and he has become proud—even a bit snobbish—about having Asperger's, even arguing the superiority of being neuroatypical. I've read the blogs of "Aspies" who were relieved to have a name for their "differentness" and to have a group to belong to. I'm less worried as a special educational professional, because children with Asperger's can continue to receive school services under the eligibility category of "autism." However, for years, California Educational Code lagged behind in its definition for this category; it relied on the old description of more severe autism

---

[38] The fifth version of the *Diagnostic and Statistical Manual of Mental Disorders*. Published in 2013.

and did not encompass the wide spectrum of higher functioning children who may need school-based services for social
skills, executive functioning, and emotional regulation.[39]

When I assess children to rule out or identify an autism
spectrum disorder, I find the *DSM-5* more serviceable than its
predecessor and much more precise than the current California Education Code description of autism. The *DSM-5*
diagnostic criteria for autism spectrum disorder are laid out
more clearly and with more specificity. The criteria span a
wider range and severity of behaviors in order to recognize
the nature of the spectrum, from classic autism to the people
who met the criteria for the former Asperger's diagnosis.

To be eligible for special education in public schools, we
don't use the *DSM*, however. A student must first meet criteria
for one of the thirteen federally recognized disabilities.[40] They
are: autism, specific learning disability, speech and language
impairment, intellectual disability, deafness, blindness, hearing
impairment, deaf-blindness, multiple disabilities, other health
impairment, orthopedic impairment, emotional disturbance,
and traumatic brain injury, according to the educational code
definitions. The disability must also adversely affect the student's
educational achievement, and finally, the student must also
require special education services in order to progress from
grade to grade.

When I discuss labels with parents, I tell them they are
important for a couple of reasons. Their child needs a label in

---

[39] In 2014, the California Education Code description of autism was updated,
but remains unspecific.

[40] As delineated in the Individuals with Disabilities Education Act (IDEA) of
2004.

order to get services in the school and services outside the school that insurance companies will pay for.[41] The other reason a label can be helpful, I tell them, is to make sure their child is being treated with the correct methods and medications.[42] It's best practice that I want to provide, of course. Another reason, which I don't generally admit to strangers, is that I have a strong need to get it right. It's my professional pride and ego at stake, I admit, but it's not just my need to be right that matters. It's the kids' need for me to be right that ultimately drives me.

Like many school psychologists, I occasionally practiced new tests on my own kids when they were little. When Matt was in elementary school, we spent a couple of hours at a card table, hunched over blocks and pictures and math problems. "Will you show me my IQ score when we're finished?" he asked, but I hedged. I never tell kids their IQ because I don't want them to hold onto a number that is not fixed but can shift around over their lifetime. I don't want to subject any child to a self-fulfilling prophecy or to contribute to expectations of any type. With their parents' permission, I occasionally give middle school and high school students limited feedback—I pull out a bell curve and use percentiles and ranges to show them roughly where they fall in certain areas.

Now that I've tested scores of children on the autism spectrum, I see a general pattern—although there are plenty of exceptions. Again, no one looks exactly the same as anyone

---

[41] This has become even more germane since January 2012, when California law changed to mandate that insurance companies reimburse families for the behavior training (applied behavior analysis) their children require.

[42] Some children on the spectrum can have atypical reactions to stimulant medications, for example.

else. I've seen overall intelligence from the retarded to very superior range; children with Asperger's by definition had to have at least average intelligence.[43] Verbal and nonverbal skills are variable; some have relatively stronger verbal ability, some have relatively stronger nonverbal ability, some have equal ability in both realms. Working memory—the ability to hold information in one's head and manipulate it (for example, solving multi-step math problems or repeating a telephone number backwards)—is usually adequate, but some children struggle with this, particularly those who have concurrent attention deficits.

The most striking tendency for children on the autism spectrum is slow processing speed. Processing speed "involves the ability to fluently perform easy or over-learned tasks. It relates to the ability to process information automatically and therefore speedily, without intentional thinking through. Faster processing speed means more efficient thinking and learning."[44] Processing speed "affects how the brain organizes information. It impacts upon a person's ability to focus on important things while ignoring less important items and is what allows the brain to shift from one activity to another ... If a person processes more slowly than the people around him, there may be negative repercussions with his level of awareness, his working memory, how he interacts with peers, and how comfortable he feels in social situations."[45]

---

[43] The *DSM-5* does not recognize Asperger's syndrome. Instead, people are diagnosed with an "autism spectrum disorder" based on deficits in social communication and social interaction as well as restricted, repetitive patterns of behavior, interests, or activities and then are rated along a continuum of severity in both categories. The three severity levels, based on how much "support" a person needs, leave room for interpretation.

[44] Cognifit.com

[45] Merridee Michelsen and Karen Vaught. Brandonhall.org

While some children score in the average range, almost all I've tested show a definite weakness in processing speed relative to their intelligence, some mild, most moderate to severe. When he was finally evaluated in high school, Matt's processing speed was way below his ability level.

Studies of language processing have shown that neurotypical children can understand speech at a certain rate (generally slower than adults speak it) and that children on the autism spectrum understand speech at a slower rate than neurotypical children. This delay may be so small it can't be observed; however, even if invisible, children with slow processing speed have trouble quickly performing simple visual and motor tasks and quickly understanding and using language —social language in particular.

Other recent research has found that children with deficits in sensory processing have trouble processing visual and auditory information at the same time. "It's like they are watching a foreign movie that was badly dubbed, the auditory and visual signals do not match in their brains."[46] This may explain why some kids with autism cover their ears when overwhelmed with competing stimuli like faces and spoken words. And why some kids I'm testing look at my neck instead of my eyes when I'm giving them directions.

Some kids with autism do not engage in eye contact, although many do. Some students have stared so hard at me that I imagined they were taking measure of my soul. A better description than lack of eye contact might be *unusual* eye contact. A psychologist wrote that Matt's eye contact was "fairly typical though it appeared forced at times and seemed as if he was looking through the examiner, rather than at her." I was

---

[46] Stephen Camarata, Ph.D., *Autism Spectrum Quarterly*. Spring 2014.

so used to Matt's eye contact or lack of eye contact or unusual eye contact that I didn't notice it anymore. The rose-colored shades of motherhood altered my vision.

I also knew about the research done at Yale that mapped eye tracking and compared people on the spectrum with a control group. While viewing film clips of emotional moments (like an argument in the movie *Who's Afraid of Virginia Woolf*), neurotypical participants tended to watch the eyes of the speakers, so their computer-generated visual scanning maps have lines back and forth between the faces of two people. The tracking of autistics' eye gaze show that they look at the speakers' mouths, the picture on the wall, the speakers' mouths, their belts, their mouths.

Once Matt and I were having an argument, and I was yelling at him about something when he started to laugh. This, of course, made me yell louder. "What are you laughing at?" I shouted.

He smiled. "Your lips look funny right now."

My assessments also include a look at the student's social thinking skills and pragmatics[47] like eye gaze, reading non-verbal cues, using facial expressions that match the situation or topic, body position when interacting, and the ability to carry on a conversation.

Parent interviews give me information about their child's sensory defensiveness. One middle school girl could not enter the kitchen at home most nights because she could not tolerate the scents of many foods; instead, her mother cooked her separate foods. I also ask parents about their child's cognitive

---

[47] I usually work in tandem with a speech and language pathologist on this area.

flexibility or whether, like Matt, they perseverate, or get "stuck" on precise language or routines. Many, but not all, students I evaluate have a history of atypical tantrums in reaction to sensory overstimulation, changes in expectations, or being denied a preferred activity. (I often want to tell parents of even-tempered children on the spectrum how lucky they are, but I can't claim to understand their family's particular challenges, which may not seem so lucky to them.) I ask about behaviors that show the child's tendency to catastrophize, or blow situations out of proportion. Many children on the spectrum are perfectionists, and this may come from a need for exactness, or it might come from difficulty rating degrees of severity of a problem. For example, if a child makes a mistake on her last math problem, she might scream and crumple up the paper, thinking her entire test was now worthless. She does not understand that this is not a Big Problem but a Little Problem.[48] She does not yet accurately rate the severity of life challenges, and this can cause excessive anxiety and lead to emotional outbursts.

I also listen for examples of black-and-white thinking, excessively literal interpretations, and difficulty with figurative language like idioms and metaphors. I also assess whether a child can take another's perspective, whether that child recognizes others' emotions and understands that others have their own ideas. I want to know how well children understand what another person is thinking or feeling by their words and actions.

I worked with a ninth grade girl once who asked me repeatedly if I was mad at her when she answered a question incorrectly or took a long time to respond. "Do you want to

---

[48] Michelle Garcia Winner.

know if I'm disappointed?" I asked her. She agreed and then frequently asked me if I was disappointed in her. She misread my emotional state occasionally because she could not distinguish degrees of emotion. When I shifted my weight in the chair, she said, "You're bored with me, aren't you?" Once, when I told her she would "just love" doing the next task, she asked me, "Is that sarcasm?"

We usually didn't schedule IEP meetings before 8:30 but were accommodating the psychiatrist's schedule. He was a busy and important man. He was the same doctor who saw Matt when he was six, and gave us no diagnosis, instead referring us to an occupational therapist to confirm our suspicion of sensory integration disorder. We had paid this man $500 for nothing, and now I was sitting across a table from him in the library at the school where I worked.

Who the hell was this doctor to come to an IEP as an expert when he still didn't know enough about Asperger's to call it what it was? His report claimed the six-year-old in question was neurodevelopmentally immature and at times behaviorally dysregulated. Fancy words for *the kid's got some delays and acts out for some unknown reason.* My report said it was Asperger's syndrome, and we recommended speech and language therapy and a social skills group at school.

Before he left the meeting early, because he was a busy and important man, he crossed one leg over the other, took a sip of coffee out of his silver travel mug, and said, "This is one of the best IEPs I've had the pleasure of attending."

I wanted to smack him. Or bill him.

• • •

One night after dinner, Spencer and I stood in line at Baskin-Robbins behind a mother and her son. When she spoke, I recognized her voice, and I looked up at her son, a boy over six feet. It was Aaron, a boy with ADHD who I'd counseled when he was in fifth grade, helping him control his anger and make friends. He was stocky like Matt and wore shorts all year long, too. I'd thought about Aaron over the years, and, with my increasing knowledge, I now suspected he had Asperger's. I wondered if he'd gotten the diagnosis from another professional after I missed it. I wanted to ask his mom; I wanted to blurt out that my son, too, had it, and I wanted to feel that special bond between mothers who are dealing with this goofy syndrome. But we were in Baskin-Robbins and couldn't talk in front of the kids. Plus I was embarrassed by my previous ignorance. I wanted to go back and do it over.

Avoid the belief that educators and therapists in the public school system are "less worthy" than private practitioners. I have had experience with a wide range of professionals (school and private practice based, including medical doctors) and I can safely share with you that there are many professionals within the public school districts who care deeply for the students and who have developed many incredibly insightful treatment approaches! I have also met many school professionals who do an excellent job understanding the diagnostic complexity of kids with social cognitive deficits. I CANNOT say that all the private professionals (educational and medical specialists) that I have met are highly competent.

—Michele Garcia Winner,
speech language pathologist, trainer, author

The day I read this quote on her website, Michele Garcia Winner became my heroine. I already respected her social communication curriculum, but her respect of us public school professionals made me appreciate her even more. And she reminds me still that I do know what I'm doing when I challenge a private practitioner's clinic diagnosis of executive functioning disorder[49] or nonverbal learning disability[50] or ADHD and OCD, instead of autism spectrum disorder. Since school staff have the benefit of observing kids in their natural environment, instead of in an unfamiliar clinic, it's entirely possible that we school psychologists are actually ahead of the cue ball on this.

At work, I often have felt overstimulated. Dozens of conversations a day stay with me, replaying in my head at night. I wake up thinking of the kids, parents, teachers, principals, speech and language pathologists, nurses, occupational therapists, and administrators with whom I work. So many people. Sometimes, I want to cover my ears with my hands and go sit in a dark quiet place.

In the car between home and work and work and home, I often do not turn on the radio. My car is my transition bubble: I leave one place behind so I can reenter the other.

---

[49] Executive functions include planning, organizing, strategizing, remembering details, and managing time and space.

[50] Nonverbal learning disability is a condition that causes impairments in motor coordination, visual-spatial perception, and social functioning.

Before my kids were born, when I worked as a predoctoral intern practicing family therapy, I admitted to a supervisor that I couldn't stop thinking about the families I worked with. It was beginning to affect my sleep, I told her. "When you're lying in bed," she said, "imagine that you are carefully placing all of your notes into a large file folder and gently putting it in a file cabinet drawer. Slowly close the drawer with your families inside, safe and protected. They'll be there when you return to open the drawer."

I still wake up thinking about kids and their parents but have become better at separating work and home. At leaving each one, temporarily, behind.

13

Reconnecting

Eleven-year-old Matt lay on his back on the floor, sleeping bag pulled to his chin, hands nested on his chest like an old man's. I was on my side next to him on the scant inches of foam pad he had allotted me. There had been two tantrums that day, and I'd been wearing my hooded sweatshirt all day, wrapping myself in its softness, in its promise of protection, in its feeling of home and safety. We both breathed slowly, deeply. He was finally sleeping, finally in the magical place that turns all children into angelic beings, softens their features, softens our souls. They are safe in their respite from reality. They are safe from us. And we from them. I was sleepy, but I forced my eyes open to watch him. As he floated away, my heart opened again and pulled him toward me.

My mother, who spent five years between her two marriages as a single parent, occasionally hollered at my brother and me and a few times spanked us. "This hurts me more than it hurts you," she said, something I couldn't understand until I became a parent and was overcome with guilt the couple of times I spanked my kids. Our next-door neighbor when I was growing up, a Catholic woman with four children, once told my mother, "A yelling mother is a happy mother." My mother had thought that was a riot.

I wanted to do better than my mother. I wanted to be part of my generation of parents who talked to their children with soft voices about their choices. I tried other methods: I dropped my voice to get their attention; I walked away; I ignored the small stuff. But when they were little, both boys routinely ignored two and three requests to stop playing with their remote control jeeps and brush their teeth. So I yelled, and it worked.

But they recoiled from my contorted, monster face. Their lower lips trembled, their expressions saying *who are you?* and when I saw that face, that look of betrayal, I hated myself.

I needed a badge. We could call it the Grump-O-Meter, and it would measure Mommy's Grumpiness Factor. Today Mommy is Happy, Cheerful, Neutral, Crabby, Grumpy, Irritated, Annoyed, and finally, at the end of the red-hot level, Angry. Then Matt, and the whole family, could check the badge—it would work like a mood ring with colors for the spectrum of moods—and they would know whether to approach or give me a wide berth.

At dinner one night, I introduced my new Grump-O-Meter idea. "From time to time, I'm going to rate my stress from 1 to 10, so you'll know when I'm irritated, stressed out, ready to blow."

Patty gave me an odd look, as if she thought I was crazy, but she didn't say anything.

"Where is the grumpy meter?" Spencer asked.

"I'm going to make one. Number one will be when I'm asleep," I said.

"Shouldn't zero be when you're asleep?" Matt asked.

"You're right. One is when I'm at yoga, or laughing. Five will be when I'm annoyed, six I'm irritated, seven I'm getting angry, ten is when I'm pounding my palms on the dining room table and yelling."

"I like it," Matt said.

Maybe he liked it because it relied on numbers, or because it would be a concrete—and visual—method, and he wouldn't have to rely on my facial expression or body language to figure out when he was bugging me. He'd have a warning before I blew.

A few days later Matt was trying to negotiate time off his most recent grounding. In the past, we had let him earn time off from grounding for good behavior. "Where am I on the Grump-O-Meter for getting a day off my grounding?" he asked.

Drawing on the social thinking work of Michelle Garcia Winner[51] and Simon Baron-Cohen's systemizing theory,[52] occupational therapist Leah Kuypers developed a curriculum called *The Zones of Regulation*,[53] much like my Grump-O-Meter, except she had the sense to get hers published. Now, teachers and speech and language pathologists and occupational therapists (and school psychologists) are using a common language with kids on the autism spectrum to help them regulate their emotions and behavior. Although I'm a middle-aged dog, I am still learning new tricks. The speech and language pathologists I've worked with most recently have

---

[51] Socialthinking.com.

[52] See *The Essential Difference: Male and Female Brains and the Truth About Autism* by Simon Baron-Cohen.

[53] *The Zones of Regulation: A Curriculum Designed to Foster Self-Regulation and Emotional Control.*

used the *Zones* with groups of students, and the teachers of children with autism use Michelle Garcia Winner's ILAUGH[54] model to focus their classroom interventions.

We still had to turn the shower on for thirteen-year-old Matt, still had to dry his hair with a towel, like we'd done his whole life. It was a ritual, and it drove me mad.

"He needs to learn to do it himself," I said to Patty.

"It's no trouble to do it for him."

"But he relies on it too much; he needs to be more flexible, to be able to tolerate a change once in a while."

Patty and I argued. Do we keep towel drying his head past puberty, or make him do it, risking his rebellion against the change?

"We need to modify the world for him," she said.

"But he needs to get along in the real world. Things aren't like this out there."

"If he was in a wheelchair, we wouldn't expect him to get around without ramps and other modifications."

This was right out of special education arguments. Modify the environment or teach the child to cope with it as it is. Patty and I were in opposite camps.

Once, when Patty was away, I refused to dry Matt's hair. I said I was too busy to start his shower. He balked. Whined. Pleaded. I walked away, and he did it himself. I wanted to push him toward flexibility, and Patty wanted to keep things the same. We fought.

I struggled over it when I was alone with him, too. When

---

[54] ILAUGH: Initiation of communication; Listening with eyes and brain; Abstract and inferential language/communication; Understanding perspective; Gestalt processing/getting the big picture; Humor and relatedness.

do I push him to do more for himself—take the bus, make his own lunch—and when is it too much for him? When does he need more time to adjust to something new?

A friend sent me a *New York Times* article about autistics not wanting to be cured, not wanting to have their behaviors trained out of them, and instead expecting the world to change for them. What nonsense, I thought. Sure, the world should make some accommodations for them, but they should also learn to adjust, to be more flexible. I wanted to push Matt to new, more flexible behavior, but I wasn't sure how much to adjust for him. Turning on the shower for him. Making the same lunch every day. Giving in or forcing him to change. The article was trying to tell me something, but I was not getting it yet.

In the mornings before he left for school, Spencer found me at the computer for a good-bye hug and kiss. I stood and lifted him up, and he often wrapped his legs around my waist even though he was getting heavy, even though he was eleven and eighty pounds and it probably wasn't considered cool for a kid his age to show so much affection toward his mom. Sometimes I turned him upside down and he did a backwards handstand out of our embrace. That was our ritual, the physical connection, the infusion he craved before leaving for the day. It filled me up, too, and I often told him he'd never be too old to hug and kiss me. "You might need to pick *me* up eventually, though," I said. Our ritual was flexible; it might have contained a hand-stand, or just Spencer nuzzling his face into my neck while I sat in the chair. Eventually we pulled apart, and he turned to go. "Is this good-bye?" I would say with flair, extending my arms dramatically, like an actress. He rolled his eyes and laughed.

My parting ritual with Matt was something I believed he didn't particularly enjoy and could do without but was routine now. When he found me at the computer, he stood next to me until I turned and stood. "Good-bye, my man-child," I said, and he put his arms out ready to tolerate my squeeze. Now taller than me, his arms reached over my shoulders. He put his arms around me ever so briefly; it was a tease more than an embrace. He sometimes puckered his lips and bent forward as if trying to reach me from afar. Maybe he liked it when I squeezed him as hard as I could and said, "I love you so much," but I was never really sure.

When he was twelve, it was Spencer's turn to go to Hawaii with me during his spring break. On our hotel room door was a housekeeping flip sign with two choices: "Refresh and Renew" and "Peace and Quiet." I considered swiping it so he could hang it on his door, requesting alone time, time away from his brother. Spencer called our four days "a vacation from Asperger's." Shortly after telling Matt about the Asperger's diagnosis, Patty and I had explained it to nine-year-old Spencer. Although he didn't really understand it then, by the time he was in high school, Spencer could spot Asperger's qualities in a clerk at Radio Shack. "That dude was hecka literal," he'd say. On the airplane on the way home from Hawaii, Spencer told me he'd like to start a summer camp for siblings of kids with Asperger's so they could have a true vacation. "And," he said, "they won't even have to do their homework on the plane."

In Hawaii, I noticed families in restaurants, on the beaches, and walking together in town. Occasionally, I witnessed flashes of muted anger between couples, between parents and children. A mom swatting a child's bottom, a couple arguing quietly at breakfast. And I realized it wasn't just our family. The idea of a blissful family vacation was hype. Who enjoyed sharing the stresses of travel—choosing a restaurant that everybody liked, finding your way around new places, disrupted sleep cycles, sunburn, diarrhea? I felt vindicated, less freakish. Our family hadn't traveled together in three years, and maybe that was preferable to being miserable together far from home. But then, after our Hawaii trip, a friend told me she was planning a trip to Italy with her kids. I was in awe. No Disneyland for us, no San Diego again. We didn't have fun anymore, or the fun times were overshadowed by the painful times. Italy with children. What a dream.

I was working on our fence, and fifteen-year-old Matt was holding the ladder for me, when a piece of wire sprung back and slapped me in the face. I put my hand over the stinging welt and whimpered. Then, the oddest sensation: his huge arms around me and his heavy head resting on my shoulder. I almost fell off the ladder from shock.

One night, Matt was in his sleeping bag–cocoon anticipating our good-night routine: I lean over his futon bed, we embrace, and I squeeze as hard as I can. But this time, I caught him before he could pull his arms and torso out of the cocoon. I snaked my arms under the sleeping bag and held him in a new version of the burrito roll we had used when he was a baby. At first he protested, but then relaxed into my arms. I was holding my six-foot one-inch baby and kissing his stubbly teenage face. I removed my arms, and amazingly, he stayed wrapped up, didn't insist on giving me a squeeze in his very particular way, too. He smiled up at me. "You're starting another ritual, you know."

Because he was now several inches taller than me, he had to lean over when I grabbed him around his waist for a hug. One summer, he tolerated three embraces in five minutes and even hugged me back. But when he got a sunburn one summer, I didn't grab him. Instead, I stood still and let him bend over and squeeze me. It was a unique feeling being the huggee instead of the hugger. Maybe with maturity he could finally tolerate our touch. Or he accepted it because he understood that embracing was one of our ways of expressing our love, even if it wasn't his way. It made me wonder if maybe his whole life he had felt as if he'd had something like sunburn.

14

A s k i n g   f o r   H e l p

A FEW YEARS AGO, I FOUND SIMON BARON-COHEN'S *THE Essential Difference*, a book about the differences between male and female brains, how women's brains are wired for communication, social skills, empathy, and how men's are wired for understanding systems. The author suggested that Asperger's is the extreme male brain. I was fascinated by this idea, and then realized a certain irony. Poor Matt, with his extreme male brain, was being raised by two women. That could either be the most unfair situation, or the best; I wasn't sure. In the book, I read examples of men with Asperger's behaving unexpectedly in social situations. Out loud, I read to Matt about the man who called a coworker fat, another who told one of his professors she was sexy. Patty and Spencer joined us, and for the first time in a long time, the four of us laughed together.

Later in the summer, I overheard Spencer and Matt debating the meaning of a word. Before it became an argument, though, Spencer said something that surprised me. "Maybe in your world it means that, Matt, but not in mine." Until now, I hadn't known how Spencer was conceptualizing all of this. He complained that we sometimes let Matt off, didn't give him a time out because of the Asperger's, but now I realized he was beginning to understand. And he was right; we inhabited different worlds.

Of course, Spencer could also hurl the word Asperger's in anger. During another argument he yelled at Matt, "Why don't you shove that burger up your ass?"

Just when I thought we might have this thing beat, that we had figured out how to avoid the tantrums, that perhaps he had finally outgrown them, just when I thought we were past the worst—cue the *Jaws* soundtrack—they came back.

"Why? W-H-Y? Do you understand English?" Matt was screaming at Patty, stomping his foot; his face was deep claret, the tears forming. He was clearly in pain, distressed, unable to control the emotions that threatened to annihilate him.

"You're stuck, Matt," I said, trying to back up Patty, not yet able to stop butting in. "You're stuck. How can you get unstuck?" I believed if Patty and I just worked together we could get him out of it. Patty had told me that Matt recently asked for help getting unstuck when he got volcanic instead of us giving him time outs. "They don't work," he'd argued. "I want to go to my room to calm down, but just for a minute or five minutes, not like when you send me in there for ten minutes or a half hour."

She had agreed to try it. I was skeptical, but loved that he had requested it. I loved that he was thinking about it when he was calm and that he might be beginning to look at his own behavior. But this time, he was already in too far. He could not hop off the merry-go-round because it was spinning too fast.

"Go now or you'll be grounded tomorrow." Patty sounded strong. She was trying so hard, and I had hope this time.

"Why, Mama? Can't you just answer that question, or are you too stupid?"

That last was too much, he would never say that to me for fear of my fury, but Patty had ignored this kind of insult before, and he probably believed he could get away with it now.

"You're grounded tomorrow," she shouted over his ranting, his chanting.

"No, Mama. Am I grounded tomorrow?"

"Yes."

"Can it just be tonight?"

She shook her head. Spencer came into the dining room, rolled his eyes, and sighed.

The loop played on: Matt screaming "Why?" and crying with deep frustration.

Patty warned him that he would be grounded another day if he didn't go to his room immediately, but he continued to rant. She seemed to be losing steam. I wanted her to go ahead and ground him another day. It would get his attention, get him to stomp into his bedroom for a long cry. It would put an end to all of this.

I also wanted her to turn and go, disengage, but she was stuck in place. They were both stuck in the loop. The loop we all knew so well. I knew it was easier to choreograph a piece than to dance it, and from my vantage point, in the audience watching this scene enacted on the stage in front of me, I could see more options. Up the ante. Take away computer. Be strong. Be the parent.

At the time, I thought I knew the best way to handle the tantrums. But after all of the years, they weren't getting better. When a method doesn't work, one should change methods. Unfortunately, we didn't know what to change to.

Matt had the whole family enraptured with his performance, his dance on the stage. I laughed at the ludicrous facial contortions he was making along with his verbal rants. My laugh let off steam for me, even when I knew it was wrong. I kept hoping something we did would snap him out of it, get him to see how absurd it was to keep repeating a word until it became unrecognizable.

I turned to go. I was not going to watch the show anymore. It was way too much attention to pay to something so non-sensical. "Come on," I said to Spencer, "Let's go do something."

I had nothing in mind, but I figured Spencer and I could get into the kitchen, close the door, and hide out until it was over. Maybe Matt would stop sooner without an audience. Patty followed Spencer and me into the kitchen. Yes, I thought, let's leave him without anyone to perform for.

But instead of giving up, getting softer, Matt was getting louder. He followed us, screaming, stomping his feet, still demanding "Why?"

Needing something to do, I filled a glass of water from the tap. I wanted to get away from the irritation, the noise—his incessant noise—that was buzzing around in my head, up-setting the balance I'd been feeling lately. It had been so much better lately; he hadn't had a tantrum in months. Once again, I had hoped we were magically past the worst. But at that moment, it struck me that we would never be past it. I was convinced we would live like this forever.

I was too annoyed to feel pity for him. Instead, I was getting angrier. And anger always trumped sadness. Before I took a sip of the water, I turned toward the door. Matt was right behind Patty, following her with his noise, his voice bouncing off the linoleum floor and pine cabinets, raking against my skin.

I fantasized about the men in white coats, the psych techs,

wrestling him to the rug and one of them jabbing him with a needle full of Haldol. I thought of Haldol—the *One Flew Over the Cuckoo's Nest* drug. I wanted the Haldol that day; I couldn't believe it, but I wanted to jab my son with a syringe full of Haldol. To shut him up. To end this.

I took a step toward Matt, and then I was tossing the water from the glass toward his face. I wanted to shock him, wake him from the trance, make him stop the noise and shake his head like a dog after a bath. I wanted him to realize his mistake, apologize, and retreat to his room to rest. Give us all a rest. Just like in a stage play, I wanted the water in the face to be a wake-up call, a shocking but harmless way to halt the scene. Just make it stop.

The water didn't reach his face; I was too far and didn't use enough force to jettison the half-cup of liquid that high. I could see its flight path during the second it was airborne, like a freeze frame, before it left its trajectory, broke apart, and landed on his shirt.

As I tossed the water, Patty said, "No, Anne," and I immediately regretted it. What the hell was I doing? This was not a drunken man who had insulted me in a bar and had earned a drink in his face. This was my twelve-year-old son who did not deserve this, did not deserve a mother who came unraveled in an instant and turned into a scary witch.

But at the same time, I believed that in some way he did deserve this, and I even regretted not getting the water right in the middle of his face, making him sputter in surprise.

"You didn't have to throw water on him, Mommy," Spencer said, and for a second I wanted to die; I was not fit to parent this child who needed someone extraordinary, who did not need someone so flawed.

But a second later, I pulled on the mask again. "Stop it," I yelled at Matt, righteous now in my anger. "Just stop it." My throwing the water had shocked him, but of course, instead of bringing clarity, it evoked his ire. He had been frustrated and angry before this, but now I had tapped primal animal rage. He was a provoked circus lion, stung too many times with the cracking whip, poked too many times with the switch.

Matt stalked to the refrigerator where I thought he was grabbing a plastic bottle of water to pour on the floor to match my stupid gesture. But it was a plastic jug of apple juice, and before Patty and I could reach him, he was shaking the jar without its lid, and apple juice was spraying onto the linoleum, the stove, and the cabinets.

During the struggle to wrest the jug from his hands, my reading glasses, held around my neck with a beaded necklace, broke, scattering beads underfoot. I squeezed Matt's wrists too hard and he broke free, railing against me, finally bringing a fist down onto my forearm. I felt no pain, only my rage matching his.

Oddly, I was not afraid Matt would hurt us. Even when Patty said, "Watch out, Anne," even when Matt's fist hit my arm, I was not afraid. His hitting me now was a fluke, a result of his trying to break away. But still it enraged me.

"Stop it!" I screamed as I slapped the top of his head with my palm. "Stop it, stop it, stop it!"

Matt stopped shaking the juice, and in the quiet, Spencer sobbed. "Stop it," he whimpered. "All of you. Just stop it."

It was then that I felt wicked. I feared I had traumatized both of my children, making Spencer witness this insane scene, frightened and powerless to stop it. I was turning them both against me; I was losing both of them.

After Matt relinquished the jug to Patty, he stalked to his room, slamming his fist on the wall every few feet.

"Great," Spencer said, "He's going to put another hole in the wall."

"One more thing for me to fix," Patty muttered.

"He can pay to have it fixed," I said. "Or just live with a hole in his wall."

I tossed a handful of rags from under the sink on the puddle of apple juice. "He can mop this up later," I said so Patty would not drop to the floor and clean this up for him.

I stepped out of the kitchen and began tidying the dining room, removing papers from the table, straightening knick-knacks on the sideboard, desperate to impose order.

Spencer followed me. "Is he going to be grounded?" he asked.

"He's grounded for the rest of the month. He has to learn to stop. He has to have a serious consequence for his behavior," I said, even though I knew there were none for mine.

Spencer began to cry again. "When he's grounded, I don't have anybody to play with."

"I'm sorry," I said. "You can play with friends." But his tears continued. "I'm sorry about this whole thing," I said, reaching for him. "Did it freak you out?"

"No," he said, "But you didn't need to throw water on him."

"I know. It was a mistake. I thought it would snap him out of it." I clapped my hands sharply and Spencer flinched. The adrenaline was still pushing me to talk and move too fast. "I wanted to get him unstuck. But it didn't work. It made it worse, and I'm sorry." I tried to bring him into an embrace, but he shrugged out of my reach and headed to his room.

I didn't want their memories to be of this moment, a monster-faced mommy, and I prayed that they would instead remember the times we held hands on the sidewalk, the times we sat close on the couch reading, the times I hugged them tightly and nuzzled their hot necks, the times I kissed their cheeks and foreheads and nose and chin and eyes and cheeks again. The times I said *I love you infinity times around the world.*

After dinner, Spencer climbed into my lap and petted my cheek. I was forgiven.

That evening, Patty and I talked to Matt in his room. We told him how long he was grounded, what he would miss. His eyes filled again with tears, and I doubted again we were doing the right thing.

"Sweet boy," I said. "You have to learn how to get unstuck. How can we help you get unstuck? Do you want to go talk with Betsy again?"

"No."

"A counselor at school?" His sixth grade teacher had called us, worried about Matt's annoying his friends. She had recommended he see the school counselor.

"No."

"How can we help you learn how to get unstuck?" I would learn a few years later that "cognitive rigidity" can be reduced by what we'd already tried—limiting changes to plans and routines and giving advance warnings when they were necessary—and what we didn't yet know about, like *The Incredible 5-Point Scale*,[55] a visual chart used by kids to help understand and control their reactions to everyday events and "Big Problem/Little Problem," a rating scale to match emotional reactions to situations and to minimize catastrophic thinking and identify "glitches," which can be worked out by staying flexible.

"I don't feel stuck," Matt said. "You're the one causing the problems."

---

[55] Kari Dunn Buron and Mitzi Curtis.

We were back at the beginning again.

I plodded up the stairs to my bedroom, slippers flapping against my soles and then snapping against the floor. I closed the door gently, although what I really wanted was to slam it so hard the glass in its upper half crashed to the floor. I wanted to make the house shake; I wanted my frustration to slam through the door, its frame, and the foundation of our house, shaking us from our center like Matt shook my core.

I had to get out of the house or I would truly go crazy—pull-my-hair-out-in-fistfuls crazy, scream-until-my-throat-turns-raw crazy, cry-until-there-are-no-more-tears crazy. I put on my shoes, left the bedroom, and walked out the front door. I drove away. For forty-five minutes, up into the hills and back down again.

Three tantrums in one weekend, each more violent than before. Matt pummeled the arms of both Patty and me, pounded on the window of her car when she left, tore a branch off a tree in front of our house, kicked a hole in the dining room wall, pulled the huge curtain at the front window off its track.

I didn't want to call the police, but Matt was as tall as Patty, and the medication had added some bulk to his frame; he was stocky and strong. I didn't want to call because I didn't want to offer ourselves up to the system and give up control over our lives. I feared two huge officers storming into our house and throwing Matt to the floor, pressing a knee into his back, and handcuffing him. I would watch this scene wanting to shout, "Be careful with him, he's just a kid." Then doctors would decide to hospitalize him, how long he'd stay, what medicines would go into his body. I'd want to tell them all to never mind. Let him go. We'll work it out. I didn't want to call the police.

I called the police.

"How do you spell that?" the dispatcher asked when I told her my son had Asperger's syndrome.

The officer, a short, burly man in his early thirties, stepped into our house and looked from me to Patty and back to me again. "We're his mothers," I said. We told him about the medicine, the psychiatrist, and the family therapist. He looked at Matt, then back at us. Matt sat silently in the reading chair next to the picture window, his eyes never leaving the officer's face. He twisted his fingers around each other.

The officer spoke calmly with Matt for several minutes and Matt answered his questions with a voice that was ragged from screaming. He had quieted as soon as I had reached the dispatcher and now appeared docile and harmless. The officer explained the process for an involuntary hospitalization, a process I knew from work. If we called again, the officer said, they'd take Matt to the hospital. And it wouldn't be pleasant, he promised Matt. For whom, I wondered.

That night, I dreamed I'd lost my right foot. I walked on a stump. You don't need a psychology degree to figure out what my subconscious was telling me.

I was wiped out, my eyes aching from crying the previous night and that morning. I wanted to sleep more. I knew now that Matt would not be able to live with us if we couldn't get him under control; he would have to go to a foster home, or a group home for emotionally disturbed kids. But the thought of him someplace where someone might hurt him made me cry more. I was so tired of trying to be strong all the time. My chest felt concave, as if it had been crushed. I was insignificant, hopeless. I wanted to curl up on the floor and sleep.

The night before, Matt pushed against me to pursue Patty with a question he was stuck on. When I grounded him for a week, he finally stopped. He cried himself to sleep, and so did I. I was fighting against Matt instead of against the Asperger's. I wanted us to fight it together, not fight against each other, but had no idea how to do it. Give in and let him do what he wanted? Trying to force him to obey was like trying to force a wild bull into a pen.

When we worked with the therapist, Betsy, she had suggested we give Matt the consequence later, after he was calm, since it only inflamed him and gave him one more thing to argue about. She helped me understand that since he couldn't say what he was feeling, I needed to figure it out and try to meet his underlying need. She suggested we talk with him about what it feels like to be stuck, use the metaphor of a train track in the switching yard. We talked about teaching him to recognize the "aura," the feelings and behaviors that immediately preceded a tantrum. We wanted to see if we could circumvent it. It all sounded so good in the therapist's office. It was another thing to use it under pressure.

In a family therapy session with another therapist years later, Matt complained that I didn't lie on the floor with him at night to cuddle and talk anymore. The last time I had, we got into an argument about his demands that I lie a certain way, that I hug him good-night a certain way, that I kiss his cheek a certain way. He begged me to resume the bedtime ritual, like Patty did with him, but I resisted. Finally I figured out what to say. "I may not be the mom who lies on the floor with you to say good-night. Maybe that's Mama's way, and we need to find another way to say good-night, to say I love you."

• • •

After another tantrum when he was twelve, and another visit
from the police, I drove Matt to Children's Hospital. I needed
somebody to do something. While we waited for a pediatrician, who would examine him and send us home, a security
guard pulled up a chair and placed it outside our door. Once
she sat, all I could see of her were her heavy work boots.
Sitting on the paper-covered exam table, Matt was quiet and
all big eyes. He didn't need a guard now. It occurred to me
that we needed her to sit outside his bedroom door when he
was raging at home. Maybe she could keep him from tossing
over potted plants, smashing framed glass. That's when we
needed someone in heavy boots.

I began to be curious—desperately curious—to know what
had caused the Asperger's. Our Asperger's and other families'
Asperger's. An impaired immune system; mercury in vaccines;
prenatal exposure to chemicals and genetically modified foods;
a genetic predisposition to unusual brain formation; enlarged
amygdala; excess testosterone; older parents; conception within
a year of a previous birth; allergy to gluten and casein. What
were myths? What was backed up by science?

I've always been fascinated by neuropsychology, or brain
science; I studied it in my master's and doctoral programs.
Having a kid with an autism spectrum disorder intensified my
interest in its causes. Studies are finding chromosomal dupli-
cations and deletions in people with autism. Although no
single genetic mutation causes autism, over a hundred are
known to make people with them more vulnerable. For me, the
studies of genetics are reassuring. They let us parents off the

hook. We mothers can stop blaming ourselves for what we might have done during pregnancy. Our kids had a genetic predisposition.

Over the past few years, when I've met with parents of kids with Asperger's, I've wondered which one of them might have passed on the genetic recipe that has made their kid who he was. Which one spoke a little too pedantically? Was there something in one's tone that sounded familiarly flat? Did one of them come off as uncomfortable in their own skin? I asked about their jobs. Computer programmers and engineers raised red flags for me. I tended to scrutinize the fathers more, since statistically they were more likely to be the link, but a couple of mothers vied for that honor, too.

In one instance, I was sure both parents had made a pretty substantial contribution. Both were highly educated and worked in the sciences. Their son was a poster boy for Asperger's. When we talked after my assessment, they both realized they, too, had many characteristics of Asperger's. "When geeks collide," the mother said, and we all laughed.

There is no prenatal test for Asperger's, like amniocentesis for Down syndrome. Nor is it visible at birth. For many, it raises its little serpent head when the child goes to preschool. For others, the signs of Asperger's are present earlier but are subtle. Matt did not show true signs until elementary school. Some students' behavior does not look atypical until they reach middle school, when social demands become more sophisticated and they can no longer hide behind labels of "immaturity" or "quirkiness."

Studies are finding signs of autism in younger and younger children, though. An early sign of developing autism was identified in babies between two to six months, when infants who would later be diagnosed with autism showed a steady decline in attention to others' eyes.[56]   These babies instead turned their eye gaze to the mouths and hands when watching their caregivers. This reminded me of Matt studying our "auras" and his time spent staring at the bank of square windows at our cabin when he was an infant.

Recent research studies[57] have suggested that the behaviors typical of people with autism are due to structural, or anatomical, brain differences. While autism has been diagnosed via behaviors, scientists are now identifying biological markers that cause those behaviors. Using brain imaging techniques, like functional MRIs, scientists have identified structural and functional differences in specific regions of the brains of children with and without Asperger's. There are also apparently differences between the brains of children with more classic autism and those with Asperger's.

Elevated levels of the neurotransmitter serotonin, thought to affect ritualistic behavior, aggression, and language use, have been found in the blood of people with autism. The gene that causes the overproduction of serotonin is being studied. Certain brain structures are smaller than typical, some are larger. Neurotypical people use a structure called the fusiform gyrus, for facial recognition. But the neurons in this part of the brain are fewer and smaller in autistic brains. When people with autism look at faces, they use a different part of the brain—the part that recognizes objects.

One study found that the brains of people with autism don't function as cohesively as the brains of people without autism, particularly when looking at faces and processing information about them. Some structures overcompensate,

[56] Warren R. Jones and Ami Klin in 2013 in the journal *Nature*.

[57] Reported in the *Journal of Autism and Developmental Disorders*, for example.

taking on the jobs of others, reminding me of a conductor-less symphony orchestra playing out of tune. It's a more fragmented system of processing information, which often takes more effort and more time than for neurotypical brains.

Some believe that impairments in the relatively recently discovered[58] mirror neurons, which fire both when we perform an action, like catching a Frisbee, *and* when we watch someone else catch a Frisbee, can explain problems with imitation, language, perception of touch, empathy, and theory of mind in people with autism. Mirror neurons allow us to understand others' emotional states.

Studies are documenting disorganized prefrontal and temporal cortical neurons in children with autism, and others are finding over- and under-connectivity between the mirror neuron system networks in adolescents, which could explain their social cognition deficits, or their ability to understand what others are thinking and feeling in response to certain events.

Other researchers[59] have found biological markers in the part of the temporal lobe responsible for social communication. When brain tissue of children who had autism was examined after death, it had an oversupply of synapses in certain regions, suggesting a lack of normal "pruning" of these connections between nerve cells. When the synapses are not trimmed during childhood and adolescence, there are too many connections among neurons, leading to an overload of stimuli and brain areas not developing specific functions. This is thought to explain why people with autism experience oversensitivity to noise or social experiences and why more than a third of people with autism also have epilepsy.

---

[58] TED talk by VS Ramachandran: The neurons that shaped civilization.

[59] Columbia University Medical Center.

Neurotypical adolescents' frontal lobes are still developing, which can explain poor decision making at that age. Studies have found a reduction of brain activity in the frontal lobe of children with Asperger's when they were asked to respond to tasks that required them to use their judgment or make inferences. That was Matt when he got stuck, when he looked like he'd lost all touch with reality, the days I wanted the *One Flew Over the Cuckoo's Nest* Haldol to make the craziness go away.

These brain differences, scientists claim, are most likely caused by nerve cells in the developing fetus ending up in the wrong location, so that the "wiring" responsible for thought and behavior is all tangled up, metaphorically. All of this, presumably, is predestined by genetics. Meaning Matt's fate was determined the second the sperm penetrated my egg. Or even before.

The reports keep coming, and I'm reminded of the parable of the six blind men trying to identify an elephant from each of their specific locations. A recent UC Davis study[60] identified antibodies in the blood of a group of women whose children have been diagnosed with autism. The antibodies target fetal brain proteins, a potential biological marker for early diagnosis (and treatment) as well as future drug development.

No study can show a specific cause in 100% of the subjects; many results apply to about a third of the group studied. It's still impossible to pinpoint any single cause for every person with autism. Some day, like the blind men sharing their inspections of the elephant, the science will all come together, and we'll understand the autistic brain in its totality.

I've read a lot of studies, and what I've settled on is this:

---

[60] Judy Van de Water, UC Davis.

our genes line up like good little soldiers in each of our cells before we are born. Each one has an important job. Some determine our hair and eye color; some determine how parts of our brain work. They're preprogrammed to go off like a choreographed fireworks display, some behaviors firing off early, some waiting for the grand finale. Schizophrenia is like a time bomb, usually hidden until a person reaches adolescence or young adulthood when it explodes.

But what about all the environmental theories? I wondered which triggers might launch those chromosomal fireworks. When I attended a lecture by a researcher[61] from the UC Davis MIND Institute, I learned that genetics alone cannot explain the 600% increase in autism diagnoses.[62] Many potential causes, like the mercury in vaccines, have been debunked by recent research,[63] but there are 80,000 chemicals that have not been tested yet for neurotoxicity. Researchers are studying PCBs and flame retardants in furniture, Teflon, BPA in plastic water bottles, and tricycline in anti-bacterial soaps. Pesticides and herbicides. Homes that use toxic flea and tick products are twice as likely to have a child with autism, but this doesn't mean there is a direct link. So far they have found associations, not causes. Immune responses may be affected by genes; however, environmental triggers are thought to be different for each person on the spectrum.

I admit that knowing about environmental exposures inflames the maternal guilt so nicely extinguished by the genetics explanations. I've always treated my dogs with flea products; I've taken long naps on couches, and I've cooked

---

[61] Clifford D. Saron, Ph.D.

[62] Identical twins are both on the autism spectrum only 70% of the time.

[63] Including The MIND Institute at UC Davis.

many meals with Teflon pans. But I want to shout, "We didn't know!" I didn't buy the more expensive organic vegetables and fruits when I was pregnant, but if I'd known pesticides and herbicides were risky, I would have. I took folic acid and prenatal vitamins before signing up at the sperm bank. I did what I could. And, I keep reminding myself, that needs to be good enough.

The newest research is looking at a "germ line" hypothesis, which suggests that eggs in a female fetus may be altered by pharmaceuticals taken by the mother during pregnancy, leading to abnormalities in that fetus's eventual children. In other words, a woman's *grandchildren* may be affected by the chemicals she was exposed to during her pregnancy.[64] It all comes back to *what we didn't know then*.

When Matt got inflexible, I didn't think about his biochemistry or his brain structures, though. I simply reacted, my body ramping up for another fight or flight, my brain struggling to recall the best way to handle Matt while my nerves constricted, my heart throbbed, my head felt light. Stay calm, my inner voice said, but my body responded all on its own, the memory of past clashes too powerful to fool myself into a Zen-like serenity.

It was anxiety, I knew, at the root of Matt's tantrums. He was an overstimulated, overwhelmed, and panicked kid, and no matter how hard I tried to remember this, I was still a victim of my own anxiety. His triggered mine and vice versa. We were all a nervous mess. I wondered if we'd ever reach a place of fearlessness, much less calm.

---

[64] Fertility, nausea, and miscarriage drugs prescribed to pregnant women in the 1950s and 1960s might have altered genes and contributed to transgenerational abnormalities like autism. See environmentalhealthnews.org, for example.

One day, I told Matt a story about our dog Mimi, who died when I was seven months pregnant with him. "I cried and cried," I said. He turned and looked at me until I met his gaze. "Maybe that's how I got Asperger's," he said softly. Years later, I would read an article suggesting that maternal stress hormones released during pregnancy are a potential trigger for developing autism in the fetus. Stress hormones passing from mother to baby, or a mother's immune responses to illness caused by stress, were believed to affect the developing brain. PTSD during pregnancy—like getting caught in a hurricane strike zone—was thought to increase the risk. I doubt that a beloved pet's death can cause the same amount of maternal stress as living through a hurricane. But who knows? I bet there are a lot of pet owners who would disagree.

I had no idea what it would feel like to drive behind an ambulance transporting one's child to a psychiatric hospital. Now I know that it feels like all of your internal organs are spilling out of you and you can't get them to go back in. I know that you talk out loud alone in the car and remind yourself not to run over any pedestrians or crash into the back of another car at a stoplight while you struggle to remember how to get to the hospital that you pass every day on your way to work. That you drive into the hospital parking lot and see other parents coming and going and you're suddenly so grateful your child doesn't have a life-threatening condition. But then you realize that it does feel like a life-threatening condition, that you won't survive his childhood.

When I had called Dr. A. to tell him about another tantrum that thirteen-year-old Matt had thrown, and the tipped-over ottoman and the bookshelf wiped clean and the

potted plant ripped out of its pot, he called for an ambulance
to take Matt to the hospital for a medication evaluation. It
would be a good thing to get a second opinion, he said. Before
the ambulance arrived, Patty left to take Spencer to his
baseball game, an ambivalent reprieve for him because he
seemed both eager to escape the scary tantrums and afraid to
leave us behind. When she returned, without saying anything,
Patty looked at me to see what was happening. "Waiting for
the ambulance," I said, and she righted the ottoman and
perched next to Matt, now sitting quietly in the easy chair. It
was St. Patrick's Day, and Matt was wearing a new green
Oakland A's tee shirt. "We're not mad at you," she said,
brushing her fingers over his knee. Her gesture made my tears
finally form. I'd stayed angry in my spot on the couch across
from him. Waiting for this to be over. Not touching my boy.

As the ambulance idled in the middle of the street, and I
waited with my car keys in my hand, I wondered if our
neighbors were watching out their windows. I was embarrassed and wanted to reassure everyone that we were okay.
Mostly, I just wanted the EMTs to finish securing the gurney
and get the hell off our block. But I didn't look at any of our
neighbors' windows. Instead I noticed buds on the jacaranda
I'd planted near the sidewalk when Matt was a baby. The new
growth hadn't been there the last time I'd looked. Everything
was so green, so new, so full of potential.

The evaluation at the psychiatric hospital, like the one the
year before at Children's Hospital, was anti-climactic. Because
we already worked with a therapist and had a psychiatrist
prescribing medication, there was not much they could help us
with. Although we feared Matt might do more damage to the
house, he had never hurt us intentionally, nor was he an
imminent danger to himself. It was a Sunday, and the social

worker said they could admit him for observation for a night. But, she said, our insurance company might not foot the $10,000 daily bill, and there was no one at the insurance company on the weekend to approve the admission. Two hours after arriving, I drove Matt home.

We were nearing the shortest day of the year, the longest night. I was about to call a supervisor at our new health insurance company to demand they quit dithering and approve our request to see a family therapist who knew Asperger's from asparagus. I wanted to tell them our house this holiday season felt more like a tinderbox than a sanctuary. I wanted to tell them that we'd be dropping the kids off at the insurance company's suburban office at the beginning of the Christmas break for two weeks. Finally, the insurance company approved our request. Our new therapist had his work cut out for him.

After another of our battles, Matt said, "See, Mommy, this is why I don't like living with you. It's why I don't even like *knowing* you."

At first, ridiculously, I smiled. Then I expelled a loud, fake laugh. I wanted to cry but I didn't. My skin was thicker now. But it was probably the worst thing he'd ever said to me. Worse than *I hate you*. Worse than *fucking bitch*. It was the measure of my complete failure.

• • •

When I told him to turn off the video game and go to bed because we had an early morning, Matt refused. I repeated myself and he put his hands over his ears and started humming. I shouted to be heard, and we were off and running in our typical race, our power struggle to the finish line. I made my usual parenting mistakes, and he acted like a kid with Asperger's. Neither of us had changed; we still got pulled into our patterns, our autistic, rigid roles, and in three minutes it was a full-blown melee with both of us shouting and him with tears dripping off his now stubbly chin. I was usually too angry for tears; those would come afterwards, when the shame and guilt rose up and stabbed me.

"You're going to have to live somewhere else," I shouted, "in a group home if you can't get yourself in control." It was not an empty threat. Although I didn't know how to go about it, I knew if I wanted to I could set that in motion. But as soon as I said things like that to Matt, I always regretted it, thought how ashamed I'd be if our therapist could hear me. But it also felt good to say it. It felt horrible and right at the same time.

"I don't care," he said, sobbing now. "I *want* to go live in a group home. It would be better than living here."

During another tantrum, I snuck out of the house and walked a mile to downtown and back. I had to get away or I believed I would have a heart attack. I would have died if I stayed in our toxin-filled house another minute. I walked and walked. I didn't want to go back, but there was nowhere else to go. I was a prisoner on my own Alcatraz.

Dr. A. prescribed Haldol, the anti-psychotic I'd fantasized about using earlier. In the middle of his tantrums, I sometimes wanted to jab Matt with a needle of the stuff to calm him down, shut him up. But the prescription was for pills and we tried them for three weeks. Matt's eyes drooped with sleepiness and his speech slowed and slurred. He fell into bed earlier every night. 8:00. 7:30. During the day, he was more volatile, had even more tantrums. The miracle drug was no miracle.

We talked with our new therapist about boarding schools. We had called the police four times. They no longer asked how to spell Asperger's. Patty and I had each taken a turn escaping to a motel with Spencer to give him and us a respite. We researched boarding schools. As in sending your kid to Oregon or Montana or Massachusetts when he's fourteen years old, and it feels like you're giving up on your kid even when a friend reframes it as asking for help.

15

T o w a r d   P e a c e   a n d   U n d e r s t a n d i n g

spec ·trum [**spek**-tr*uh* m] *n.*

a broad range of varied but related ideas
or objects, the individual features of which
tend to overlap so as to form a continuous
series or sequence.

I LOVED OUR NEW THERAPIST. IF OUR PREVIOUS THERAPIST,
Betsy, had been a life raft, this therapist was a hospital ship.
But I despised him the first time he referred to Matt as
disabled. I worked with kids who were disabled. The special
education laws I worked with every day were written for
students who were disabled. I did not have a disabled child.

In addition to books on psychological theories, the new
therapist had literature on his shelf, books of comics, poetry.
He came up with more metaphors than any therapist, or
writer, I'd ever known, and he was so right on with his comments, I quickly trusted him. Patty and I met with him weekly,
and the boys took turns to talk about what was bugging them.
He practiced Floortime[65] with some of his younger clients, but

-----

[65] A system developed by Stanley Greenspan in which parents and therapists
interact with children in order to help them develop basic thinking skills:
engagement, interaction, symbolic thinking, and logical thinking.

with Matt, he told us he wanted to develop a relationship. That sounded a little too much like traditional psychotherapy to me, but I respected his experience and was willing to follow his lead. Equally or perhaps even more importantly, he would help Patty and me understand Matt and find better ways to relate to him. True, this is how good therapists of any theoretical orientation should work with children, but we needed an advanced course: how to parent a kid with Asperger's.

Once, I joked about my own autism kicking in, and our therapist suggested that maybe we're all on the autism spectrum, just in different spots. I liked that idea. We're not truly diagnosable, but maybe from time to time we move around on that spectrum—sometimes pulling away from people, going deeper into our autism, sometimes pushing ourselves back into the world.

I've fought my perfectionism for a while now, almost daring myself to make mistakes and trying not beat myself up over them. I can be rule-bound, too much of a "good girl," and I could stand to let my reliance on morality ease up a bit. On the other hand, I am hyperattuned to others' feelings and what they might be thinking. I pick up on the subtlest of cues. A slight change in a stranger's expression makes me alter my behavior in order to keep them comfortable. I'm an over-empathizer, overappeaser, and overpleaser, and my ability to take other people's perspectives is definitely intact. I crave change to stay interested, and the most enjoyable part of my career is the social interaction. Therefore, I'm afraid, I'm not on the autism spectrum.[66]

---

[66] I've found the online self-evaluations for Asperger's syndrome almost comical and definitely ironic. Asking people with compromised social thinking to judge their own social behavior is like having someone who is tone-deaf tune their own piano.

There are some who feel the brain differences found in people with autism serve an evolutionary purpose, that an autistic brain is actually superior to a neurotypical one. Some believe that people on the high functioning end of the autism spectrum have a brain that is better suited to the specialized, highly focused roles that our evolving world is demanding.

What Was Normal

Brothers bickering. Even taking a swing or two, our therapist assured us. Parents nagging about too much computer time, worrying about their kids' grades and marijuana at the middle school and the day they start to drive.

What Was Not Normal

Wondering every day what could happen to make me weep again, if I'd have to call the police, if someone would get hurt, really hurt. Wanting to run away from home at forty-nine.

To Matt, "cuddle time" did not include touching. It meant lying on the hardwood floor next to him before he fell sleep in his sleeping bag–cocoon–burrito roll. Sometimes there was talking, sometimes not. Patty had more patience for this ritual than I did. I complained that I was too tired to lie down at 9:30, that if I did I'd get too sleepy to get any work done afterwards. I knew I should have done it anyway—I feared there wouldn't be much more time that I'd be invited. Our therapist agreed and said that, for Matt, cuddle time equaled intimacy time. I started lying on the floor and willing myself to stay awake. It didn't always work, but at least we were together.

A Few Other Things the New Therapist Taught Me

1. When we don't give Matt an answer, he feels left out, injured.
2. Instead of consequences and punishment, we should talk about what he did that made us upset, made the dog upset, made the family upset.
3. Matt wants intimacy, he just doesn't know how to get or show it.
4. Teach Matt that the Spanish homework is like a crossword puzzle. You can skip a few clues and circle back to them.
5. Matt can't tolerate spaces and endings. We need to help him have a plan for after his friend goes home and he feels lonely, something we have set up beforehand.
6. Matt's questions mean he needs company in curiosity. If we don't know the answer, we can make some guesses with him.

Just before Matt's fourteenth birthday, Spencer and I were whispering in the kitchen when Matt walked in. We stopped and looked up, caught. "What are you talking about?" Matt asked. "What to have for dinner," I said quickly, hoping to move on, get him to leave the room again so Spencer and I could continue making plans for Matt's birthday. Matt stared at my face, and I knew the lie was right there, visible. "Did you just lie to me?" he asked. I struggled with my choices. Should I keep up the ruse to get him to go away, or do I come clean? I decided that since we wanted him to be able to read faces, it was important that I gave him correct feedback. "Yes," I said. His eyes filled with tears. "Don't lie to me," he said.

Few children with Asperger's lie, even to get out of
trouble. Lying is not logical; it's against the rules, it's not
concrete and true but an abstraction and false. Those children
with Asperger's who have figured out how to lie usually can't
figure out when others are lying because that takes an understanding of subtle communication cues like facial expression
and tone. It also requires taking the other person's perspective,
and if you can't imagine why someone would lie, then it's
going to be hard to tell that they are.

One Christmas vacation, Matt shouted something from the
living room.

"What's wrong?" I asked.

"It's annoying," Matt said, his voice rising in intensity. My
gut hardened, and I prepared for battle. "Spencer moved my
bookmark."

"Yes, it is annoying," I said. "I'm sorry it happened."

"He *took out* my bookmark," he screamed.

"I know. It is annoying, but that's all it is. It's not earth-
shattering; it's annoying." At the time, I was coming up with
my own Big Problem/Little Problem strategy, but mine wasn't
visual and we didn't know that we should be using it for a
variety of problems in order to teach him the difference.

He slammed his fist on the wall. "Yes, it is earth-shat-
tering!" He slammed his bedroom door behind him and
turned immediately quiet.

After an hour of reading comics and listening to music on
his headphones, he emerged as Dr. Jekyll. Ready to decorate
the gingerbread house with Spencer. I hovered during the
raising of the gingerbread walls and its exterior decoration.
"Keep talking about your plans," I said. "Get agreement before

you do anything." It felt like we were back in preschool, where I learned to help kids resolve conflicts.

Matt added icing. "Are you okay with that?" he asked his brother.

Spencer stuck candy where they had agreed it would go. Before starting the project, Matt had designed a 4×4 grid, had even drawn the placement of the gumdrops with alternating colors.

"Matt," Spencer said, "you like it very organized."

"Yes, I do," Matt said.

Those days, yoga, walking in the hills, and writing kept me sane. When I was on break from working in the schools, I wrote draft after draft of a memoir, a mystery novel, a three-act play, and a collection of essays about two moms raising two boys. I ran off to Maine twice a year to work on an MFA in creative writing. I edited essays for a parenting newsletter, organized writing groups, taught writing at a bookstore. My MFA writing mentor's praise, and my writing days alone in my studio, saved me. Then, in the womb of my free-writing group, I wrote about the painful parts of my life: "Writing about this makes me feel like I'm putting myself back together." When I read this aloud, someone moaned in acknowledgment.

In first grade, Matt and I wrote a manuscript about a boy getting ready for school. Matt sat on his small chair next to my swivel office chair and dictated the story of Jason who rides the bus to school, buys lunch at school, and has a dad, all things out of Matt's experience. It was written in the style of an Arthur[67] book, Matt's favorite book series at the time.

---

[67] A series written by Marc Brown.

In sixth grade, Matt and his friend Derrick, the only kid who still came to our house for play dates, cowrote a hundred-page children's novel manuscript. They returned to their elementary school and read excerpts to the fifth grade class, and the kids laughed in all the right places. Matt typed up an evaluation form. *What is your favorite part in the book? What would you add or change?* We four parents of the coauthors were asked to take turns editing the manuscript, and Matt asked my advice on finding an agent.

A friend of mine heard this. "Wow. He's doing what you do."

When he was about fourteen, Matt was spending a night with his uncle and called us the next morning at eight o'clock. "I forgot to take my pills last night," he said. "What should I do?" The Seroquel seemed to be working better than the last medicine. Either we were in another good period, he was working really hard on his behavior, or the medicine was working. We could never be sure which it was.

Patty and I were both on extensions when Matt called. "Take it now," we said in unison.

"Okay."

"You're such a good boy," I said, missing him now that he'd been gone sixteen hours. "We love you."

"Okay," he said. "Bye."

His senior year in high school, when Matt decided to stop the medicine, he told us he resented our forcing him to take it when he was growing up. "It didn't do any good," he said. "And I didn't like how it made me feel." When I look at photos of him taken during his teens, his puffy face and doughy body makes him so look so different, so not like my child, that the hook of guilt tugs at me again. When he went to college, Matt *lost* the freshman fifteen pounds instead of gained it like many do. Now, at six-one, he's just the right weight, slim and muscular from biking to his job.

Did we do the right thing by medicating him? I console myself now by remembering that we did everything we could, consulted with doctors and therapists about alternative therapies, read books, searched the youthful Internet. We were unsure and scared and did not take decisions like medication lightly. But we were desperate. Medication was a last resort, right ahead of sending him away to live somewhere else during the explosive years.

I can forgive myself now because we went with what we knew at the time. Would I do things differently had I known what I know now? Of course. I would have used the wealth of information that has come out of recent years of research and clinical practices; we might have tried more specific therapies and behavior consultants; we would have attended parent support groups and trainings so we could learn how to make Matt's life easier, so we could shape our behavior more than trying to shape his.[68]

However, even now, when I work with families with kids on the spectrum, I hear of physicians prescribing stimulants for their attention deficits, which can cause side effects more serious than loss of appetite and difficulty sleeping. Some kids have experienced psychotic thinking and have been hospitalized to keep them safe and to modify the chemical cocktail that is prescription medication. It's still an inexact science, and not all practitioners are up-to-date yet on best practices in pharmacology, so families continue to struggle with these decisions.

---

[68] I believe that *Uniquely Human: A Different Way of Seeing Autism* (2015) by Barry M. Prizant, Ph.D., with Tom Fields-Meyer, will help families raising young children on the autism spectrum.

•   •   •

At breakfast on Valentine's Day, thirteen-year-old Matt gave
me a card from the store that read, *From your favorite kid. I bet
you didn't know I knew, huh?* His moments of intact perspective-
taking amazed me.

As we all ate our cereal that morning, I read an Ogden
Nash Valentine poem to the whole family. It was a funny poem
because of its use of opposites, and after the stanza that read *I
love you more than a wasp can sting/And more than the subway jerks/I
love you as much as a beggar needs a crutch/And more than a hangnail
irks*, Matt interrupted. "But a wasp can only sting once." We
hushed him so I could finish the poem, but he continued to
perseverate on the wasp's stinging capability. When I finished
the poem, Patty and I explained the subtlety to him. It was the
pain of the sting, not the number of times the wasp can sting.

That evening, Matt raced inside from playing and headed
straight to the kitchen. "Are we having Cactus?" he asked
Patty. Cactus Taqueria was his favorite burrito restaurant.

"Yes, you're having a treat tonight," she said.

"But is it Cactus?"

"You're having a burrito, yes."

"But is it Cactus?"

By this time I had joined them. "I think he needs a clear,
concrete answer," I said, but I wasn't sure anyone heard me,
the tension was already so high. I wondered if Patty had had a
couple of glasses of wine before we got back; when she drank
she became even more obtuse when she spoke. I usually
resented it, but now it infuriated me.

Patty was cooking what looked like crab cakes, a special
treat for her and me, and we'd all seen the bakery box in the
fridge marked "No Peeking." She'd spent some time on this

dinner. But Matt still needed his question answered. "Did you get Cactus?"

Finally she said yes, and he looked relieved. But he immediately asked, "And root beer? Did you get the root beer?"

"No," Patty said.

"Why not?"

"Because we have other treats. I bought a special dessert for tonight."

He shook his head and mumbled, but when she asked him to set the table he did.

We sat at the table, our Valentine's cards stacked on the hutch. I hadn't taken the first bite of my crab cake or asparagus when Matt began to shout.

"You cut my burrito," he said. "Why did you cut my burrito?"

Patty had needed to check which burrito was his, with refried beans, and which was Spencer's with black beans, so she'd cut one in half.

"It's written on the burrito, Mama! Why didn't you just read it?" Patty explained that the last time we got burritos from Cactus Taqueria, we'd had to open the burritos to see which was which. "That was the only time!" he said. "They always write on the burrito. You could have just read it! Why did you cut my burrito in half? I can't eat it now."

It was so clearly an Asperger's moment, I was actually calmed with the knowledge. We could handle this. He needed to know we heard him, he needed Patty to apologize, he needed us to not shout at him to shut up and eat it, but to empathize with his disappointment. I started to reflect back his feelings like a good psychologist, and it felt briefly like I was working with a client instead of my son. I was so detached, could see it all so clearly, and could empathize with him so perfectly, that I never became angry, just a little sad for him.

But as soon as I began to tell him I understood his disappointment and asked him how we could help make it right, Patty tossed her fork onto her plate. "I can't stand it anymore." As our primary chef, she had had a hard time with the boys' rants about food, moaning about eating veggies, complaining that they didn't like the new casserole she'd made. Her feelings had been hurt over and over, and we'd tried the tough tactic; together we had warned them if they made comments they would be sent from the table without dinner. It had been better lately, a few scrunched-up faces when eating new foods, but few comments. That night, though, when Matt couldn't tolerate the change in his burrito, she reached her breaking point. She stood and shouted, "I can't stand this. I don't want to be here with this family."

I raised my palm. "Wait a minute, Patty," I said. "We can work this out." But she was already out of the room, heading for the front door. Spencer looked panicked. He screamed, "Mama, wait! It's not your fault!" Then she was gone. I imagined she'd walk around the block and come back in time to finish dinner, or for dessert at least.

Matt began to cry, real tears of deep disappointment over his burrito. Spencer's face was crumpled. "Where's Mama going?"

"She's a big girl. She can take care of herself."

"But she needs us to tell her it's not her fault."

"That's not your job." My tone was too harsh, I knew. I was angry with Patty. Yes, she was allowed her feelings; I'd walked out before too, but Matt's problem now was so clearly not rudeness but an Asperger's moment. An Asperger's crisis.

"I don't have a job!" Spencer said, his voice angry.

"I know you don't. I mean that Mama needs to take care of herself."

"But we could help her."

I glanced at Matt, who was wiping two streams of tears off his cheeks. "Why did she have to cut my burrito?"

My two sons.

"Matt, you're stuck. Mama made a mistake. She feels bad, very bad. But it's over now, what can you do to make it right?"

"It's not over. It's still cut." With this knowledge, he cried harder, stood, and left the room. He retreated to his room, shut his door, and sobbed.

I looked at Spencer. "This is Asperger's, do you know that?"

He nodded, solemn now.

"It's not his fault," I said, and he nodded again. "He needs our help."

"I know. So does Mama."

Matt cried for ten minutes and then joined us at the table again. He picked up the burrito. "It's cold now." His eyes were red, swollen. His heart was broken, I realized, and then I was aware of the irony. It was Valentine's Day.

Near the end of February, the four of us watched the Winter Olympics on the couch. There had been no tantrums for several months. But then, watching TV together, thirteen-year-old Matt—now six feet and taller than Patty and me—began to chatter and banter with Spencer, laughing at his own jokes. He left the couch and lay across the ottoman in front of us. He poked our toes and laughed, and Spencer laughed too, egging him on. Matt was tired, I believed, and watching television or movies before bed had been problematic in the past because when it was time to get up off the couch and get ready for bed, the transition was sometimes too much for him.

I told Matt to be quiet many times, but like an exhausted

toddler, he got more wound up. He continued making noise, and finally I sent him away. He refused and we were treated to a typical tantrum—screaming, tossing the ottoman over, and scattering books and magazines. Standing next to me, he was now my height. I slipped on my clogs because I was afraid he'd throw one of them if he spotted them lying there. For the first time, I was truly afraid of him. I found my cell phone and turned it on. "I will call the police again," I said and couldn't believe we were back to that point. So far past *1-2-3 Magic*. He was yelling; his cheeks were pink, and spit was forming in the corners of his mouth. I turned off the TV and sent Spencer to bed. He cried. "I'm not used to it," he said about the return to tantrums, and I realized he was right. It had been a long time. And we all hated their return.

One night, I was trying to corral Matt and Spencer into their bedrooms to get ready for bed, playing traffic cop in the hall outside the bathroom. Spencer had to pass Matt in the bathroom doorway; it was a tight squeeze, and Spencer leaned to his left to avoid bumping Matt. But Spencer brushed against Matt's forearm just for an instant, and Matt immediately recoiled and elbowed him in the side. "Don't push me!" he cried at his brother, who, shocked at the outburst, began to cry.

"Whoa!" I shouted, thrilled that I had seen this, finally had witnessed what must happen so often behind my back. "Spencer, I'm sorry Matt elbowed you; go upstairs and get ready for bed. I'll be up to cuddle with you soon." I threw my arm out to prevent Matt from leaving the hall. He was still whining and rubbing his arm where it had been brushed. "No. You stay right here. I saw exactly what happened. You need to hear this."

"Your body just sent you the wrong message," I said, my voice raised more in excitement than anger, but he was on the defensive.

"I didn't do anything wrong!" he shouted. "Spencer pushed me, so it was okay to hit him back."

I skipped the part about it never being okay to hit back; he'd heard that a million and a half times. "Your body sent you the wrong message," I said again. "It sent your brain the wrong message. He didn't push you, he brushed against you. Lightly."

But Matt was shouting, so I shouted at him to stop yelling at me, and then I was plugging my ears like he sometimes did because it was too loud, and at the same time I was yelling over him. "You will hear this," I insisted. I would say it over and over until he understood, until he truly understood.

"What did I say to you just now?" I asked.

"I don't know."

"Your body sends you the wrong message."

"Okay."

"What did I say?"

"I know my body is sensitive!" he shouted.

He understood.

We took Matt to a new social skills group. They made paper-clip chains to represent links in a conversation and tossed a ball back and forth to keep a conversation going. Don't drop the ball. Ask personal questions. The speech and language pathologist met with us parents after each session, telling us what they had worked on and what we could do at home to remind Matt to use his new skills. Every week, when Matt and I got in the car to go home, he said, "What's for dinner?" and I said, "No. You say, 'How was your day, Mommy?'"

"How was your day, Mommy?" he asked.

"Good, but tiring." I paused, waiting for a follow-up question about my day.

"Okay," he said, "What's for dinner?"

One weekend, Matt asked me to take him to Jamba Juice, and when I refused he started to rev up. He asked "Why?" in a pre-tantrum voice, and before I launched into three reasons to support my answer, I simply told him, "Because I don't feel like it." But that was not enough; it left much too wiggle room for argument, and I finally understood he needed something more. I'd recently read about perspective-taking in a book, how kids on the autism spectrum have trouble imagining what another person is thinking. "It's like when I ask you to go on a walk with me and you say you don't feel like it." He thought about it a minute and when he finally said "Okay," I breathed again.

Another day, I chased Matt through the house to get a hug, him laughing at my pursuit. When I stopped and shot my arms out in their robot hug position, he didn't detour around me, but approached my docking station. Some days he gave me a squeeze. I always held on longer than he did, but he was finally tolerating my hugs. Matt leaned over, put his arms around me, and squeezed briefly. He only hugged when leaving for school in the morning, undoubtedly because it was part of his routine. But every day when I got home from work and found him hunched over a bowl of cereal or the computer keyboard, and I patted his back or squeezed his shoulders, he wriggled away from my touch. It needed to be on his terms.

•   •   •

During the summers, I insisted on physical exercise. We walked to the movies and insisted the boys walk to and from play dates and the computer game store. Eventually, they got jobs refereeing soccer games and umpiring baseball games. I loved walking places with Matt alone; he was more talkative and calm. When I teased him or talked in a silly way, he looked at me sideways with his beautiful braces smile. He eventually outgrew saying, "Oh, Mommy," but he still smiled with what looked like love.

One evening, Matt and Spencer and I watched a movie on our old TV in its new location in an entertainment center. I warned Matt that the seating arrangement would be changing, and he pulled up the ottoman so he could sit with his long legs extended. I moved it closer to me so we could share it, and he balked. But I insisted and he accepted the need to share the ottoman with me. Still, he squirmed and adjusted his body to avoid touching my feet and my throw blanket. Baby steps.

Watching him flick his knuckles on hard surfaces made me want to cry. He really did have a type of autism; I saw him do milder versions of the stimming movements the kids at work did. One night, he came into the living room and sprayed his aerosol sunscreen across the room. I lost it, screaming at him, "How could you do something so stupid?" All I could see was his acting like an idiot, his disregard for other people, his autism. When he acted goofy, I think it bothered me so much because I was beginning to understand he was truly disabled—

or *differently* abled—and he had a condition he would not grow out of, and he might always embarrass and infuriate me. Having the label "disabled" had begun to help me when Matt acted immaturely or provocatively; differently abled allowed me to accept his goofiness and not try so damn hard to change it.

16

School Days

WHEN HE RETURNED HOME FROM ELEMENTARY SCHOOL
every day, Matt took a snack from the pantry into his
bedroom and closed the door.

"Why do you think he's doing that?" I asked Patty one day.

"Maybe he needs to get away from the stimulation of
school."

I thought of what he negotiated every day: the noise of
the hallways, brushing against kids passing classes, listening to
teachers and students talk, concentrating on assignments,
writing notes and responses and essays, filtering essential from
inessential information, formulating ideas, talking in class, and
negotiating the social periods. Tasks that most neurotypical
kids manage every day. Maybe Matt needed a break between
the school demands and the noises, smells, and touches of home.

Eventually he joined us in the living room, eating Spanish
peanuts from a blue plastic bowl.

"What did you do today?" I asked.

"Went to school."

I waited a minute for elaboration, but he was done.

"Nice talking with you, dude," I said as he headed outside
to shoot some baskets.

•   •   •

I took Matt to work with me on one of his school holidays, because I wanted him to see the kids I worked with and about whom I often talked at home. In one of the preschool class-rooms for students with autism, the kids sang a song about the days of the week. "Today is Friday," they sang. "All day long!" Matt looked at me and stage whispered, "No, it's only Friday for two hours!" I was immediately embarrassed, worried his comment would be overheard. It wasn't until later that I appreciated he had used sarcasm, that indeed, even if it had been a rude use of it, he had learned sarcasm. When he was younger, he had looked perplexed at or frustrated by our sarcasm. But I can't take credit for thoughtful teaching of the concept; he probably learned it when I got angry with him and said something like, "Oh, yes, I really love your behavior right now!" and he replied, "No you don't; you're yelling at me." And I would have replied, "I'm being sarcastic!" thus stamping that subtlety of language into his knowledge base. Such a skilled school psychologist–mom.

My Worries About Middle School

He wouldn't have anyone to eat lunch with.

He'd get picked on.

He wouldn't be able to find his way around the school of 900 kids.

He'd get suspended for doing something stupid.

The Reality

He ate lunch with the boys from fifth grade: the math geeks, I called them.

He was so tall no one messed with him.

He loved carrying his multi-section binder, got all his homework done on time, and made the Honor Roll the first semester.

He got suspended for doing something stupid.

When I answered the phone one afternoon, someone was crying so hard on the other end, at first I thought it was a prank call. The sobbing continued, punctuated by gasps for air. It was almost nonhuman, this anguished cry. "Mommy," he said, and I knew it was Matt. My heart slammed into my gut.

"What's wrong, love?" I asked. At least he could talk. He wasn't dead, and it couldn't have been life-threatening, or someone else would have been calling. But something horrible must have happened.

"Mommy," he started, but his crying took over.

"I…"

Sob.

"Got…"

Sob.

"Suspended!"

"Oh my God!" I nearly shouted with relief. "You really scared me. I thought you were hurt. Slow down and tell me."

"I put the window on Kenny's head."

"You did what?"

"I accidentally closed the hall window on Kenny's head." His voice was returning to normal now that he was concentrating on explaining what had happened.

"Is he hurt?" I imagined a concussion, a hairline fracture, or a crushed skull. I imagined having to face the boys' parents in the hospital, in a courtroom. I would defend my son. He didn't mean to, I'd say, sounding just like all the parents who couldn't admit their kid was a bully. But mine really wasn't. He was a bull in a china shop, but not a bully.

"No, he's okay. But I have to come home now."

"All right, sweet boy. Let me talk to your teacher."

She explained it wasn't serious but they wanted to make an impression on Matt. He needed to stay home the next day and write down what he had done that was wrong.

Patty and I had threatened the boys with a home jail term if they were ever suspended from school. "We better not get a call like that," I'd said one night when Spencer told us about two classmates fighting. "You will be in your rooms until you're twenty-seven," I had promised.

Matt must not have known what to expect from us; this was the first time he'd been in any serious trouble at school, and deep humiliation settled into his voice. He would spend the suspension in his room with nothing to do but read. And this would be enough of a punishment. He needed no lecture from us; his remorse was so great he cried again when he got home. "I didn't mean to hurt Kenny," he said over and over, genuinely stumped over how pinning his classmate's head on a windowsill had caused such a disturbance.

At times like this, I scolded myself for my past impatience. Why couldn't I remember how badly he felt for misbehaving? For a time, all he had needed was for one of us to say, "I'm so disappointed," and he would turn to quivering liquid. I'd used this tactic when he was younger, but over time, as he'd gotten more inflexible and explosive, we'd fallen into the shouting and punishing trap. He needed help understanding his friends' perspectives and how to read their faces, body language, and tone of voice, not more time alone in his room.

Parent-Teacher Conference

"I'm concerned that he doesn't feel empathy for other people."

He cries during The Incredible Journey *when the cat dies.*

"He's not taking responsibility for his actions."

He admitted to hurting Kenny.

"He doesn't show any remorse."

He says he's sorry when he spills his milk at the table.

"He treats other people," she hesitates, "in a mean way."

He's always been a good kid at school.

"He hit one of his classmates today."

He probably thought he was being playful.

"He has trouble judging people's body language and the nuances behind what they're saying."

Now that *sounds like him.*

Since Matt got good grades, and teachers usually praised his enthusiasm, Patty and I had decided to wait until it became necessary to tell his elementary school teachers about the sensory integration disorder. After he slapped another student on the back and the boy fell and scraped an elbow, though, we came clean about the Asperger's. "Now I see it a little differently," his teacher said. "Maybe he didn't mean to push so hard." She continued, "His teachers might like to know at the beginning of the year; then we'll understand his behavior better. There's really no stigma."

But I knew differently. In the teachers' room at my school, we laughed and groaned at kids' behaviors and that of the wackier parents we had to deal with. We were jaded and judgmental; our comments could have been offensive if heard out of context. It was all part of letting off steam, like doctors' morbid jokes during surgery when the patient is knocked out.

There was indeed a stigma with those diagnoses, and it skewed expectations. Some teachers may have expected less of Matt, let him get away with more. Some teachers may have been harder on him when they knew what was going on. We were not sure which way to go.

"Did you mean to hurt Kenny?" I asked.

"No!" He was indignant. *How could I even suggest it?*

"Were you trying to be friendly?"

"No." If nothing else, he was always honest.

"Were you being funny?"

"Yeah. I wanted to make him laugh."

"But your teacher said his face was getting red, and he was angry with you for hitting his back so hard."

"I didn't know."

Patty joined in. "Remember when I told you the expression 'a bull in a china shop'?" she asked. "You're so strong, you have a lot of power, and you have to control your body so you don't hurt people. Like when you jump on our backs and we yell at you for doing that? We know you're being loving, but you have to show it another way."

"I'm not being loving. I'm just jumping on your back."

I wondered whether this would be the beginning of him not understanding nuance at school, too. I feared this was the end of Matt's "passing" as neurotypical outside of home.

When I shared with the teachers in the lunchroom that my son had been suspended, they all laughed. I did, too. I was not just a school psychologist to them now; I was a mother, too.

Patty and I met with Matt's seventh grade science teacher because his test grades were sliding from As to Cs. I listed the

Asperger's challenges: abstractions; inferences; drawing conclusions; ambiguity. How he struggled writing the conclusions of his last science report. How he might need some extra help to keep his grades up. "It's developmental," she said, straightening stacks of papers on her desk. "Perfectly normal. They're all challenged right now."

I wanted to tell her I knew the cognitive shift at this age was developmental; I'd been assessing it in kids for over twenty years. I also wanted to tell her, *Lady, you have no idea what developmental looks like around our house.*

What I Had Imagined When Matt Started High School

1. He would have a bunch of friends, and they would come over and ravage the pantry.
2. He would introduce me to his girlfriend (or boyfriend).
3. He would win achievement awards.
4. He would sleep in on weekends.
5. He would letter in a sport.
6. He would be editor of the school paper.
7. He would go to a better college than I did.
8. He would be a happy, well-adjusted kid.

The Reality

1. He had one friend who came over once or twice a month when invited, but never called or invited Matt over.
2. He couldn't name the other kids in his classes.
3. His grades after freshman year fell from As and Bs to Ds and Fs.
4. He could not get out of bed to get to first period.
5. He rowed on the crew team for part of a year, got hurt, and quit.

6. He stopped writing creatively.

7. He could not get through his homework without falling apart from the stress.

8. He was an overwhelmed, raging, crying mess.

The accommodations on the 504 plan[69] we'd developed with a school team in middle school were no longer keeping him afloat. We requested an evaluation for special education eligibility from the school district. It was denied.

The crew season ended, and the father of one of the girls sent out links to a video he'd set to music. It was a gorgeous montage of photos and video clips of the kids rowing in unison, lined up in their neat rows, shooting through the water. It was a video yearbook with photos of the kids at regattas working and resting, carrying boats, and snoozing under the team's canopy. Boys and girls, varsity and novices, laughing together, embracing each other. A popular song I didn't know pulsed with the rhythm of the races and rest periods. I couldn't get over how beautiful the kids were, the boys and girls, even though they were really just gawky teenagers. I recognized the boys I'd shuttled to practice, the girls from Matt's elementary school. Girls cuddling, boys with arms thrown across each other's shoulders. I waited for a photo of my son to appear but it never did. Not even a shot of him standing next to a group of kids, his favorite spot—the

---

[69] Section 504 of the Rehabilitation Act and the subsequent Americans with Disabilities Act, which specify that no one with a disability can be excluded from participating in federally funded programs or activities, including elementary, secondary, or postsecondary schooling.

satellite orbiting the social system. He had been to every practice and all the regattas except the final one when he was injured. My son was not there, even though he had been there.

Sophomore year, Matt no longer got out of bed for first period, and eventually began missing second period. Dr. A. changed his medicine again. We left him overnight at a hospital for a sleep study, where he texted us a photo of him with a cap of wires on his head like a freaky robot. By the end of the year, Matt's GPA had slid down to the level that force colleges to reject students, but he'd already passed the high school exit exam, and gotten a decent score on the SAT, so the school district argued that he didn't need any formal accommodations or special education. But he got no homework done, failed most tests, and punched more holes in the walls. We all continued seeing his therapist, Patty and I brainstorming actions until our brains hurt from the storm. We had him evaluated at the university psychology clinic, presented it to the school district, again requested that he get some help organizing his work, studying for tests, writing papers, and relieving his stress, and again asked for an evaluation for special education.

I now felt the pain of scores of parents over the years who were desperate for help for their kids and who requested special education. Some students, like Matt, appeared to manage at school and then at home lost their composure, melted down, or showed signs of anxiety or depression, but since they were able to access the school curriculum and earn adequate grades, they were not eligible for special education. The law requires a disability to *adversely affect educational performance*, but this standard was changing over time as administrative law judges were finding that children's social achievement was equally as important as their academic achievement.

I knew that Matt met special education criteria for autism and that he needed help at school. We had the advantage of behind-the-scenes experience in this very field, but still Patty and I had to convince the school district staff, first that Matt had a true (mostly hidden) disability and, second, that the general education program was not meeting his needs.

After attending probably a thousand IEPs over the years, the thought of my own son's terrified me. At Matt's IEP, the school staff presented their reports. Matt is a delightful, social student who is getting adequate grades with no need for special education services, they said. Nothing about his wearing Giant's tee shirts and shorts without a jacket every day of the year. Nothing about his inability to write a three-paragraph essay, or his obsessive line editing as he wrote first drafts. Nothing about his inability to finish all his homework or study for a Spanish test. Nothing about his falling apart at home as a result of stress he experienced at school. Nothing about his sensory defensiveness. Nothing about the baseball statistics in newspaper sports pages that he had piled in high stacks around his bedroom or his inability to get out of bed for school. Nothing about his having only one friend who rarely called. Patty and I exchanged glances. They had no idea who our son was. No idea what he needed. The battle had begun.

When Matt began his sophomore year in high school, I got to meet my heroine, Michelle Garcia Winner, at a talk she gave to a parent group in a bookstore in Walnut Creek. Sitting on one of the folding chairs set up in the Mystery section of the store (irony noted) with a dozen other mothers and a couple of fathers, I pulled out the tiny notepad I carried in my purse and, as Winner talked, I filled pages and pages of notes that I would eventually use to fight for an IEP for Matt. Finally, finally, finally, someone understood exactly what my kid needed. Finally someone else knew, and was saying it publicly, that many kids on the spectrum don't have *mild* social and learning difficulties, they are simply *less obvious*. When Winner said that grades were less important than emotional health, I underlined it in my notes and put a big star next to it. It was exactly what I tried to convey to Matt's school about his hidden disabilities. Winner was the first to articulate for me so clearly that kids with Asperger's learn differently. Their grades might be average but their social problems often *cause* learning problems. She put into words what Patty and I had seen Matt struggle with at school and at home, and what was getting worse for him every year of public school.

Winner was the first to help me really understand that social *thinking*, not social *skills*, is the true need for kids on the spectrum, or for any kid with what I have come to call "social communication" difficulties. She told us that social *skills* require social *thinking*; we have to be able to understand how others are thinking before we can interact with them in an expected manner and that children on the spectrum must be taught this skill directly since it's not hard-wired like it is in neurotypical children.

The teaching begins with eye contact, if necessary, so children know where to look for facial clues. Then they must be taught joint attention, or the ability to follow a person's eyeballs to figure out what they might be thinking—a skill developed by neurotypical infants. The long-term goal is the ability to accurately guess the thoughts, emotions, and inten-tions of those with whom one is communicating, a process that is intuitive for those with neurotypical brains, and again, must be taught directly to those with atypical ones.

Social communication encompassed the pragmatics problems I'd seen in Matt and the kids with whom I worked. I'd already let parents know that social rules change as kids age, that children in elementary school can often get by with parallel play and goofy interactions, but that by the later grades—and middle school in particular—they begin to stick out, their peers start noticing their quirks, and they no longer seem to know how to fit in anywhere. Winner also made me realize that the rules change for students all through their school day, forcing them to adapt to many different people (teachers, custodians, secretaries, lunch staff) in many different situations (classroom, playground, lunchroom, bathroom, office). How exhausting! No wonder Matt lost it at home; he was frazzled by all the demands—sensory, emotional, and social—all day.

Students need to be taught that others have thoughts about them based on their behavior and that if you want others to have normal thoughts about you, you must put normal thoughts into their head instead of weird thoughts. If they have weird thoughts about you, they won't want to interact with you. And since most children on the spectrum do desire interaction, they must learn to behave in socially *expected*[70] ways instead of *unexpected* ways. Since what you do affects how I feel, if you do something unexpected, I feel weird about you. In the end, it's the *teaching about thinking* that leads to improved social skills.

---

[70] In Michelle Garcia Winner's social thinking vocabulary, expected/unex-pected takes the place of the terms appropriate/inappropriate when teaching children about their behavior.

• • •

Michelle Garcia Winner recommended that IEP goals focus more on emotional health and managing emotions over academics and more on "social smarts" than "science smarts." She believed that IEPs should be functional and should prepare the student to work in society (with groups) and get the skills to hold a job. By the time they leave for college, kids need to be able to create a peer network, self-advocate for their learning needs, use public transportation safely, organize their belongings, solve unforeseen problems, and perform home-based chores. They need to learn how to study and what to study and when. This is what we wanted for Matt in high school.

Winner also spoke to us desperate parents about some of the academic challenges that smart kids on the spectrum can have, just what Patty and I were seeing in Matt as he got older and the school curriculum morphed from memorization of facts to inferential reasoning and higher abstraction demands. Less literal interpretation, more understanding of figurative language. Less black and white, more gray. Less predictable, more fluid and changing. Less cut and dry, more mushy and wet. Dangerous territory for a kid who was cognitively rigid.

From Winner's talk, I was reminded that language is an abstraction in itself, since words represent objects, and it requires moving from literal to abstract understanding, which is often slower to develop in children with autism spectrum disorders. Because of this, they can have difficulty with reading comprehension when they have to start reading for more than facts and information, when they must identify events that advance the plot of a story or foreshadow future actions, or when they must understand a character's motivation or perspective by locating the dialogue and other nuances that describe that character.

And since written language depends on reading, which depends on understanding pragmatic language, which needs to be directly taught (whew!), students need to be taught social thinking before they can get their thoughts down on paper. Matt took hours to start a five-paragraph essay for school. He knew a lot about the subject but did not know how to get all the details into a cohesive whole even when we encouraged him to verbally articulate what he wanted to write. Matt, like many kids on the spectrum, often did not understand *why* he was required to write down his ideas. "If they ask me, I can just tell them," he argued. He could not, as Winner said, "write so you can understand my thoughts."

One of the mothers in the audience raised her hand. "What helps them organize their thoughts and get them on paper?"

"Tons of visual cues, visual supports," Winner said. "Three-by-five cards, visual maps, webbing. Abstract information needs to be laid out visually."

Also, students must understand figurative language (idioms, metaphor, sarcasm) in milliseconds, not in the seconds or minutes it may take their brain to make sense of a word or phrase or the tone in which it was presented. Because of this, most standardized tests are not sensitive enough to pick up this disability in students on the spectrum. These kids can score high on standardized, multiple-choice achievement tests because they are measuring purified information, with much of the subtlety stripped away.

The formal pragmatic tests that speech and language pathologists administer have no time limit so they don't measure the ability to quickly interpret social language. Kids

on the spectrum can often figure out the correct—or expected
—response when sitting in a room with one adult, but they're
lost when in a group of peers engaged in rapid-fire crosstalk.
Many also have trouble talking with just one other peer
because of a lack of conversation skills. Winner advises we
observe how students work in a group: do they participate, can
they collaborate, do they act bossy and take control? Watching
for social chitchat in group work is another, better method of
identifying social communication problems.

Matt's problems with writing can also be explained by the
central coherence theory:[71] many people on the autism spectrum have difficulty conceptualizing whole chunks of information; instead, they attend to details and rely on their (often
excellent) rote memory. This thinking style makes them miss
subtle contextual cues, so they cannot understand the main
idea in a conversation or passage in literature. Perception of
the Gestalt (or unified whole), theory of mind (understanding
that others have different thoughts, desires, and intentions)
and working memory (the ability to hold information in mind
and manipulate it) are often weak. Temple Grandin explained,
"I am unable to hold one piece of information in my mind
while I do the next step."[72]

Knowing this now explains a lot; I wish we'd known it all
those nights we sat with Matt when he got stuck correcting his
spelling, grammar, and setting up the word processor's font as
he wrote each labored sentence.

•   •   •

---

[71] Uta Frith.

[72] Temple Grandin. "My Experiences with Visual Thinking Sensory Problems
and Communication Difficulties."

A pediatric neuropsychologist diagnosed one of our students with a nonverbal learning disability, a diagnosis with a huge overlap with Asperger's.[73] In her office, she found him eager to engage with her and using good eye contact, so she ruled out Asperger's. When I observed him in his classroom, on the playground, and in the cafeteria, I saw a boy who did not engage with his kindergarten peers without a teacher's facilitation. I saw a boy with strong visual-spatial skills who monopolized conversations, talking only about the most recent superhero movie he'd seen. And when I saw him walking the perimeter of his classroom on his tiptoes while running his hand over every surface at waist level—including his teacher's abdomen—I knew. When I spoke with his mother before the IEP, she said she'd suspected it was indeed Asperger's. "I wish we'd had you evaluate him before the neuropsychologist," she said. I'm still ashamed to admit how great that felt.

For five years, I walked on weekend mornings, early, my neighbors' newspapers still secure from the dew in plastic bags on front steps. It had started as a training regimen for a sixty-mile fundraising walk, and it morphed into a workout and therapy session. Next, I found myself checking out streets where I might like to live on my own when the kids left home, if Patty and I decided to end our marriage. Heading east, I climbed into the hills, which overlooked the sapphire bay and glittering San Francisco skyline. For a time, I explored paths and steps between streets, taking novel routes and pretending I was on vacation exploring a new town. But when times were

---

[73] Children with nonverbal learning disability have a unique profile on cognitive testing, and children with Asperger's tend to show more restricted interests and stereotypical behaviors.

hard at home, and I could get out of the house and move my body and breathe air not poisoned with our hateful words, I stuck to one route. Every Saturday and Sunday, I walked toward the hills to Euclid, turned north and hiked the curving street to the top, then followed the Grizzly Peak ridge until it was time to turn on Spruce and head down. An hour up and a half-hour down. I knew exactly what time I'd return home. I didn't stray from my path.

Walking my route was automatic, making it a comfort. I didn't need to think about where I was going or make decisions along the way. Walking my route was hypnotic, allowing me to sink into a Zen state, a clarity-seeking place. Instead of clearing my head, though, I often got lost inside it, wandering its tangled paths. Kids I was assessing at work. The parents who were making unreasonable demands. What I was writing. When I could get to my writing studio next. What was waiting for me at home. Whether or not Patty and I would end up little old ladies together as we'd imagined for so long.

I was aware of the push-pull between routine and adventure. On the days I took a new route, I needed the stimulation that wandering off the path brings and which I craved from time to time. I couldn't imagine taking the same route every time no matter what. It would have bored me to death. It would have been too autistic.

But there were times—those hard times—when I wanted to block out the world, and I needed the comfort of sameness, the freedom from weighing options, from exploring newness, from moving outside my egocentricity. On those days I stuck to my path.

• • •

For two years, I had worked at the elementary school with the boy named Nathan who had sensory integration disorder and who toppled chairs and hid under tables. I tried to help teachers figure out what he needed to get through the day, I sat next to him under the table, held him screaming on my lap in the hall. When he bit my wrist, I didn't get angry. It was my job.

Then I took a leave of absence to write full time for a year, the year we got Matt's diagnosis of Asperger's, and the break gave me cherished time to nourish my creativity, working on a memoir that I needed to get out of my system. When I returned to the school district, I was assigned to a preschool for children with communication delays and autism spectrum disorders. Everything and everyone was new to me: school buildings; principal; teachers; aides; speech and language pathologists; custodians; school secretary; bell schedule; a dozen yellow buses lined up three times a day; classrooms full of cute, miniature students.

I was glad for the change but all the newness was exhausting. Names of staff and children to remember, preschool assessment materials to learn and use, a new driving route to work, new parking rules, a new office to settle into, new schedules to memorize, school bells at a different time. New vocabulary and teaching methods. Applied behavior analysis.[74] Sensory regulation. Discrete trials.[75] So much newness. Now, I try to remember the unsettled feelings, the bombardment of information and stimulation and expectations of a new job when I see kids on the spectrum react to new settings. And I

---

[74] Applied behavior analysis is the application of behavioral principles to increase or decrease targeted behaviors. When I was in college, I studied behavior modification by identifying the ABCs (antecedent, behavior, consequence).

[75] A teaching technique that breaks down skills (for example, tying shoes, reading) into small components or steps.

understand better how it must feel when they have to move from one grade to another, move from elementary school to middle school, and move from middle school to high school. Everything so new, it might feel as if they're on a rocking boat and they can't get their footing, can't get stabilized.

Sometimes, at the preschool, I felt as if I was in the movie *Invasion of the Body Snatchers*. About half the students had autism; the others had communication delays not caused by autism, so I never knew which kids would sing "hi" as they passed me in the hall and which kids would stare right past me, as if I wasn't there.

Nathan's mother called me from time to time to give me updates. Over the years, three of us school psychologists had evaluated him, and all of us determined that he didn't qualify for special education since his achievement was so high and the law says a disability has to be adversely affecting educational performance.

But the more experience I got with children on the spectrum, the more I suspected that Nathan had Asperger's. When I called his mother and asked if I could evaluate him again she sounded tearful. "Oh, yes, please," she said. The speech and language pathologist and I worked with Nathan and conferred. It was Asperger's, and it was adversely affecting his social and emotional functioning. His IEP team recommended an inclusion program for middle school, and that fall his mother called me. "He's doing really well," she said. "Thank you so much for sticking with him."

Although I regretted my tardiness, it felt as if I was making amends.

•   •   •

In a technical writing extension class at the university, I wrote a twenty-page guide to identifying Asperger's syndrome for my forty-three school psychologist colleagues. One of the other school psychologists and I presented a workshop on autism spectrum disorders to our staff. I did not want one more kid to be misdiagnosed or to be ignored by a system that did not yet meet their needs.

Then, for over a year, I led a task force where a dozen of us school psychologists researched law and policy, discussed the successes and failures of the district's education of kids with Asperger's, and finally, presented recommendations for special education eligibility and appropriate services for these kids who were showing up in greater numbers every year. After twenty-five years of work as a school psychologist, I knew that I, like my colleagues, had missed identifying students on the spectrum. My work was beginning to feel more substantial.

Perhaps I still don't see it, such is the implicit nature of denial, but today I believe it was not denial I suffered before we got Matt's Asperger's diagnosis. It was ignorance. I had accepted the sensory integration disorder diagnosis and looked no further. Denial was when a mother of a student at one of my schools raised her voice at me after I suggested we assess her third grade son because of his lack of friends, his tantrums at changes in routines, and his all-encompassing interest in the migration patterns of monarch butterflies. Denial was her telling me that her son did not have Asperger's because her mother, a psychologist, had ruled it out. Even though there were three men within one generation on their family tree diagnosed with Asperger's.

We believe what we need to believe. Or what we know.

Reading about conditions, even studying them in graduate
school like I did, does not guarantee we can see them when the
condition is sitting right in front of us. I think most good-
enough parents, like me, ask: *How could I have understood my kid
better* and *Could I have done a better job?* When I think back on this
time, I remember the nagging guilt I felt over my ignorance,
my inability to fix everything at work and at home, my
imperfections. I was hard on myself. But over the years, the
guilt has softened into acceptance.

You'd think parenting would get easier for every
generation; we have the benefit of scientific studies and the
experiences of so many others who have gone before us. But it
does not. Every first-time parent has no job experience. We
learn on the job with little instruction. We make mistakes, we
fail, and we succeed.

I should have known what it was. I'm over that. *Could I have
done more?* Like most mothers, I'll probably never be over that.

I evaluated a three-year-old boy in his home. The boy checked
me out like any three-year-old warming up to strangers in his
house. He peeked in the living room and ran away, then came
back for another look. He said hello when his parents asked
him to, and at first nothing looked amiss. But when he placed
a soldier figurine on a shelf, walked across the room, and
stared at it from the corner of his eye and flapped his hands as
if to shake off water, I had an inkling. After interviewing his
parents, and spending an hour with the boy, I gave them my
impression. He had high functioning autism. They were
disbelieving; the boy's aunt taught children with autism and
she had told them he was not autistic. "A milder form," I said,
trying for gentle authority. My mouth was suddenly dry. "It's

more difficult to recognize when kids are high functioning," I said. And I knew I'd come full circle. I could have been speaking to myself.

Soon after one school year ended, I attended a conference presented by Australian psychologist Tony Attwood, an expert on Asperger's. Three hundred women, and maybe a dozen men, filled the seats in the huge hotel convention room in Sacramento. After each vignette or statistic he shared, there were head nodding and smiles. In front of me, a woman put her hand on her neighbor's neck and rubbed it gently. The neighbor wiped tears from her cheek. Confirmation. Affirmation.

I wanted to cry, too, when he suggested the best ways to deal with kids with Asperger's, and I was reminded that what I was doing was all wrong: shouting, imposing overly zealous rules, expecting Matt simply to change because I demanded it. But I hunched over the table and took detailed notes to bring back to work and home.

1. For a person with Asperger's, the overriding priority may be to solve a problem rather than satisfy the social or emotional needs of others.
2. People with Asperger's must be taught that "neurotypicals" need to be told they're loved and need to be hugged.
3. A client's mother asked her teenaged son why he never told her he loved her. "I told you when I was ten," he said.
4. Many clients with Asperger's complain about hugs and don't understand why people must come up to them and squeeze them.

5. Asperger's isn't always noticeable in preschool.
6. People with Asperger's are very sensitive to emotional atmospheres and take on other people's upset.
7. They focus on an *action* (being bumped) and may not understand a person's *intention* (accident vs. attack).
8. People with Asperger's have a one-track mind, like the tracks of a train going on only one path.
   Neurotypicals can drive off-road vehicles, metaphorically.
9. Under the anger of tantrums is sadness and anxiety. Tantrums and breaking things help release negative feelings.
10. The level of stress for a person with Asperger's is directly proportional to the number of people present.
11. Emotions often flood people with Asperger's, sort of like a panic attack, so they may overreact to negative experiences.
12. It's more effective to change behavior through logic instead of punishment. Cognitive therapy can be helpful with managing and expressing emotions.

When I started working as a school psychologist in 1985, and for the first twenty years, I recognized one or two students with autism each *decade*. In the five years between 2005 and 2010, when I worked at a public preschool for children with communication delays and autism, I evaluated a child every other month newly identified with autism. More recently, between 2010 and 2015, I saw a student every month who ended up fitting the profile. I've come to the point where I don't want to see the signs and really, really want it to be something else. Immaturity. Delay in development. Language disorder. Learning disability. Anything but autism spectrum disorder.

It's not easy to tell parents that their child is on the autism spectrum. I know it's not what they want to hear, even when they're desperate to know why their child is so confusing to them, sometimes so far from the tree. When I throw out my arms wide to show them the spectrum, my shoulder aches with tendonitis, reminding me of the years of traveling among schools, pulling my backpack on wheels behind me. I've been doing this a long time, but I still empathize with the families I get to know. Even if I did not have a kid of my own on the spectrum, I would empathize so much I'd wear myself out.

It's almost impossible now to leave autism behind when I go home from work. Even with Matt off at college, I run into someone on the spectrum, hear about someone on the spectrum, read about someone on the spectrum, or guess that someone is on the spectrum every day. Someone's brother, husband, uncle, father, nephew, cousin, next-door neighbor, and occasionally, their mother or sister or niece, has been diagnosed with an autism spectrum disorder.

Because it's hard for many parents to believe me when I tell them their child has all of the signs, I sometimes slip into our conversation my almost thirty years' experience. And when I feel it will help, I mention my own kid. Some of the fathers want hard facts. Percentages. "Where exactly is my daughter on the spectrum?" one asked me, his wife rolling her eyes at her husband's persistent data seeking.

I wonder how they see me. I'm older than most of them now. Do they respect me as a professional, like they might a doctor? Or do they need to dislike me for what I've said? Some parents challenge my findings. "His doctor says it's not autism, so we'll go with her assessment," a few have said. At those times, I remind myself that even if my report is not immediately understood or appreciated, it might sometime in the future be of some help to the student, perhaps in college or later.

I remember when Dr. A. gave us Matt's diagnosis. I was not angry with him. I was surprised, confused, and ashamed that I hadn't seen it. But I was also relieved, and I see that emotion in many of the parents I work with. Relieved to know what it is—relieved that we hadn't caused it with bad parenting. Relieved that we could now do something about it. Many of the parents I have worked with most recently had had an inkling, so when I tell them, it isn't really news.

Each year, I've worked with a few more students who have already been diagnosed with Asperger's or autism spectrum disorder,[76] so their parents have asked me simply to confirm it and help their child get special education services with an IEP. When parents and doctors already suspect an autism spectrum disorder, it's easier for me. I still have to do the assessment, but I can relax and enjoy the student as I take notes, jotting down what he needs at school to make his life easier and to help him learn instead of wondering how his parents will react when I call them in to discuss the testing results.

The day after the meeting with the psychologist who insisted our student had OCD and ADHD, and was not like Rain Man, I got an email from the mother of Nathan, the boy with the sensory integration disorder diagnosis who we finally figured out had Asperger's a few years earlier. These are the

---

[76] The *DSM-5* (2013) dropped Asperger's disorder in favor of autism spectrum disorder with three levels of impairment. The social and communication categories were combined and sensory integration issues were added.

moments that balance the work for me, the moments that allow me to report for duty for another school year.

"*As Nathan promotes from 8th grade…it is simply amazing how he has grown by being in the Asperger's program. We are still learning what makes Nathan tick, but having the opportunity to provide for him at school without me being there is priceless. Thank you.*"

17

———

L e a v i n g

IT TOOK EIGHTEEN MONTHS, A SPECIAL EDUCATION ATTORNEY, and formal mediation to get Matt's school district to pay for his last two years of high school at a private school for students with learning disabilities and Asperger's. The public school staff still felt he was making "grade appropriate progress" even though he was failing two classes and not getting to school before third period.

But there was one more hurdle. The private school didn't accept everyone who applied. They wanted kids who could be successful in their program. I wrote the most important letter of my life, introducing my son's potential, his goodness, and our pride in him. Our therapist, the hospital ship, spoke with the director. "I didn't list his strengths," he told us, and for a moment I feared we might be doomed. "Instead, I told her how I felt about Matt, about our relationship." I wasn't terribly hopeful after this either, worrying it was too touchy-feely. He told us why he approached the recommendation in this manner; it was another opportunity to help us understand how our son sought and formed relationships, how kids on the spectrum challenge our notions of what relationships are. He believed that relationships with people on the spectrum can

teach us about the nature of human relationships, something
I'm finally beginning to understand.

At the beginning of his junior year, Matt left his hometown
high school and the kids he had known since preschool. He left
the campus he had memorized from maps handed out on the
first day of school. He left familiar teachers, schedules, and
routines. And he left behind the expectation, our family's
expectation, that he would graduate in a red gown in a huge
outdoor amphitheater, the three of us cheering for him, Patty
and me exchanging tearful glances with the parents we'd met
all those years before at the preschool.

The private school did accept him, and they let him make
movies in lieu of writing some papers. They let him wear one
earphone hooked up to his iPod, because listening to music
helped him concentrate and stopped him from chatting with
his neighbor. The school offered a calculus class for two
students, he and Molly working as a team on problems. Matt
hated to write out the steps ("It's so obvious, why do I need to
write it?") so he dictated and Molly wrote them out. But he
still got low-grade warnings for not doing his English
homework. "I hate reading and writing," Matt said at his IEP,
smiling at me, his writer mother. "Touché," I said at what I
saw as another of his age-appropriate separation maneuvers.

We applied to the Regional Center of the East Bay[77] for
help at home. When frustrated, Matt was still swiping entire
bookshelves clean with an arm, sending books flying to the
floor. He still had trouble getting up in time for school in the

---

[77] Regional Centers are California nonprofits that contract with the Department of Developmental Services to provide or coordinate services to clients
with developmental disabilities.

mornings no matter how many alarm clocks he set, what incentives we provided, what consequences were imposed. He was not washing his hair more than once a month, and although he could navigate the city bus and BART systems by checking their schedules on his cell phone, Matt would not have known if someone asking for directions was a tourist or about to pull a gun and rob him.

The Regional Center accepted him as a client, and his caseworker set us up with a behavioral specialist who came to our home to help get him up in the morning and reduce his emotional outbursts throughout the day. It was not a miracle cure, but Matt would try things suggested by the behavioral therapists that he would shun and deride if they had come from us. And it gave us a reprieve, breathing room, the space to back up and begin to let him go. We'd been so intertwined with him and his moods, we still did not know how to best parent him. And even after a couple years of therapy, Patty and I still fought about it: the same old argument, the same old polarity. Do it for him to save the peace or push him to do it himself and risk the inevitable explosion.

But Matt was a tough case for the behavior therapists. They, too, became frustrated with him when he got stuck or rigid. In their two hours a week, they felt what Patty and I had felt for all these years. After a year of their assistance, Matt still threw tantrums when frustrated. The walls of our house were bare, all the artwork stored in the basement, and Patty, now retired, stopped repainting the patched spots. She was waiting until he was out of the house to fix it up again.

The Regional Center held a team meeting with social workers, nurse, occupational therapist, psychiatrists, behaviorists, and the three of us. After our caseworker presented the background, and the team asked us questions, someone men-

tioned a referral to a group home. There it was—what I'd
fantasized about all those years. This is where we'd ended up,
and it felt right. He needed to go live somewhere else where he
could get his behavior under control, where he'd realize how
good he had it at home, and maybe the appreciation would set
him straight. I glanced at Matt sitting quietly, his eyes tearing
up, and at that moment I felt deep sadness and shame. How
could I even consider sending my kid away?

But I could consider it, and for the first time I knew I
could do it. I'd been afraid for some time that he'd go too far
and hurt one of us. Why should we wait until that happened;
why not do something now? And apparently the professionals
around the table agreed with me. They nodded, commented
about how his behavior was traumatizing our family. There
were openings at one place; he could go this week.

The three of us rode the elevator down to the lobby
without speaking. My throat was dammed with guilty pain. In
the car on the way home, we stayed quiet. We'd come to the
end of the road.

Asperger's and I have an uneasy, ambivalent relationship. I do
not love Asperger's, have never loved it, and am pretty sure I
will never love it. Asperger's has from time to time stolen my
child from me, has stretched my relationship with him to the
brink of irreversible damage too many times. Like a kid-
napper, it has taken my child, and I have wanted to provide
any ransom that will get him back. It has forced my son to
work harder to manage almost every detail of his life, and I
have resented that. At one point, I believed Matt might eventually turn it all into a spiffy college essay proclaiming how his
Asperger's syndrome had made him tougher, more resilient,

and more deeply connected to us, his loved ones, because of the hardships we'd all endured. Maybe someday he will indeed feel that way, but to me now, that thesis is nothing more than a sappy movie of the week.

I anticipate my feelings will change as he grows into adulthood, because he and I can already talk about The Asperger's as if it is something outside of him, something with control, but not total control, over him, something he is learning to battle when required, accept when prudent, and finesse as necessary. He appreciates the qualities that Asperger's may give him, like his contentment with being alone (something I discovered when I was much older) and his ability to focus intently on what is important (to him), a quality that he believes comes from his "not needing as much variety as most people."

We can now joke that The Asperger's is stuck on a topic, or The Asperger's wants to trash the house, or The Asperger's is not so good at keeping a conversation going. But more and more, I see less of The Asperger's and more of My Son. I recognize the skills that Asperger's gives him, and the ways he has learned to circumvent the challenges it causes him. I am finally done cleaving and have begun the process of integrating.

One of the tasks of parenting is letting go, but I was letting go of more than I ever thought I would have to let go of. I was letting go of expectations. I had let go of imagining Matt at an Ivy League college even though he was smart enough for one. I imagined him, if he could manage college at all, at a smaller place where he wouldn't get overwhelmed and lost in the crowd, where they'd keep an eye on him. And, I thought, an active Geek Club wouldn't hurt.

I wondered if my boy would ever find a mate. The four of us once watched a terrible movie called *Mozart and the Whale*. The cloying script annoyed me, although it was interesting to see the similarities between the protagonist and Matt. The character's apartment was lined with stacks of newspapers because he liked to save things. The week before, I had finally demanded that Matt recycle the stacks of newspaper sports sections that lined the walls of his bedroom. "Fire hazard," I said. *Too weird,* I thought.

In the movie, the girlfriend cleans up his apartment and throws out his shower curtain, and the guy freaks out. The three of us gave Matt sidelong glances. He smiled. "That's like when Mama moves things in my room," he said. "That gets me mad."

Would my boy date a woman with Asperger's? Would he marry a woman (or man) with Asperger's? Would anyone put up with his quirks, his brain freeze? Would he live alone by himself? Would he be content or lonely?

One evening when both boys were in high school, Patty added cheese to the dinner biscuits for a change. "What's this?" Matt asked when he bit into one and hit the band of cheddar inside.

"It's nice to have a variety of foods," Patty said. "It makes life more interesting."

"I don't like variety," he said, smiling. "Life is interesting enough."

I craved change; I needed novelty to stay interested. My family made many moves when I was a child, living in several houses in several states. I was grateful that Patty and I did not have to move, that we could keep that much stable for Matt. But maybe moving so much had helped make me flexible.

Maybe Matt needed the pot stirred up occasionally, so he'd know how to handle more unpredictability and know how to get through the peaks of discomfort when routines changed, when his rituals were threatened. When he lived on his own.

One day in the car Matt and I were talking about Buddhism—he'd learned in school that Buddhists don't want anything, don't *have* to have anything. After a brief pause, he said, "It's the opposite of Asperger's."

My first year as a school psychologist, I learned that one of the veteran school psychologists had begun her career in 1957, the year I was born. She put in her thirty-plus years and eventually retired, and I was impressed with all those years of work. Now, I was working with school psychologists who were born in 1985, the year I started as a school psychologist. And I was now bumping up against that thirty-year mark. It was a weird, karmic timeline.

When Matt was fifteen, Patty asked him where he envisioned himself in ten years. "Here," he said, "with you and Mommy."

I read somewhere that if kids with Asperger's don't leave home for college or a job after high school, they likely never will. We never followed through with the group home placement. Following the meeting with all of the professionals around the table, things had begun to shift. Attending the new school for his last two years of high school took away some of the stress on Matt, and therefore on us. He also made a developmental leap around that time that eased our lives somewhat. We watched him struggle to control his emotions and talk through problems. His ability to take our perspectives noticeably improved.

Still, when he was a junior in high school, Patty and I
began looking at transition programs—supervised living situations to help with independence training: cooking, laundry,
using an alarm clock—in case he needed it in order to get out
of our house. At the open house for the College Internship
Program, we listened to stories about young adults going to
community college, getting part-time jobs at Jamba Juice,
bowling on Thursday nights. There were therapists to help
with socializing, filling out applications, managing money. We
toured the apartments, and I could imagine him there in a
couple of years. But walking through the halls, peeking into
apartments, and imagining our boy leaving made my gut churn.

When I worked at the School for the Deaf at the beginning of
my career, I first became aware of the grieving process for
hearing parents of children with deafness.[78] Because their
children were "far from the tree," many did not know how to
communicate with them and were frightened by the prospect
of raising a child so unlike them. Later, as I worked with
families of children with other differences or disabilities, and
before I had my own children, I saw the pattern of grief. I
could only partly understand then what it must be like to have
one's hopes and dreams for one's child altered. I saw their
shock, disbelief ("That can't be right"), resignation ("We knew
something was wrong"), anger ("You don't know what you're
talking about. How dare you!"), and sadness ("Will he outgrow
it? What will his future be like?"). Occasionally, I saw relief
and hope ("I'm glad to have a name for it; now what do we do
about it?").

---

[78] Deaf parents of deaf children may not see deafness as a disability and may
not experience grief at all or in the way that hearing parents do.

The day I realized that Matt's path was no longer my own, that it branched off and rambled and wiggled—and was not necessarily a straight shot to college, job, marriage—was liberating for me. I think this happened when he left his public high school for the private one, and when I knew that although he had the smarts for a university, he might not have the executive functioning skills to succeed at one. This was reinforced when he called home during his first year at the state college complaining of a head cold and in a panic from missing two days of classes. He was ready to quit and come home that time and several others, mostly when he got behind with assignments. During those crisis phone calls, I breathed deeply and slowly and spoke softly. Because I no longer had a stake in his success at a traditional college, I could just listen, remind him there were other options, and let him figure it out, as painful a struggle it might be.

During his senior year of high school, Matt refused to keep taking his medicine. When he went cold turkey, I called Dr. A. "It's all right," he said. "Just call the police if it gets worse." But it didn't. For a while it stayed the same. And then, it got better.

A friend told me about her brother-in-law, a grown man recently diagnosed with Asperger's. He worked as a software developer, lived alone in a high-rise condominium in a big city, and competed in bicycle distance races on weekends. He did not date and had only one true friend. He spent more time with his bike than with people. "Is he depressed?" I asked my friend. I couldn't imagine a life without a constellation of friends, associates, and colleagues. My life was full of people who recharged me. I'd be lonely, and I worried my boy would be lonely. "Oh, no," she said. "He's perfectly content. I think he gets stressed when he has to be around too many people. If he's ever depressed, it's because he has to miss a bike race because his company is having a picnic."

Later that day, as I sat in traffic, I understood something so large, a quiver of current raced from my heart and lodged in my heels. I recognized the familiar tingle of sadness, but it was mingled with a surge of hope. My son's life was not my own. He was from me, but he was not me. What made me happy did not necessarily make him happy. And in a flash, I could see my son in ten years. Not in a hospital under a suicide watch, or living in the transition program we'd checked out, but in his own place doing whatever it was he loved doing. I could see him heating up the same frozen dinner every night, and I could hear his voice over the phone when he said, "Oh, Mommy. You worry too much."

For four summers, Matt went to a filmmaking camp in Berkeley. In the fall of 2008, when his group's film was screened at the Berkeley Film Festival, our family bought tickets at the UA Theater and cheered loudly. At his small high school, he took a filmmaking class both years, and in his senior year, he made a short documentary about autism, interviewing a young man with autism, as well as Matt's own therapist and previous speech and language pathologist. He also interviewed one other professional: a school psychologist who happened to be his mother. This film screened at his high school's film festival, held one morning at Oakland's Grand Lake Theatre. As I sat in the cavernous theater watching my son's final film from high school, I finally knew that he would be all right.

• • •

In the fall of Matt's senior year, Patty and Matt and I took a long weekend and drove the five hours south on I-5 to Ventura to visit a film school he was interested in. Patty and I had begun to notice a change in Matt since he had turned seventeen. He still got anxious about ambiguity and frustrated when things didn't go his way, but his tantrums were milder, shorter. He began waking up in time to get to his first class at his new school. And there was a noticeable shift in his ability to examine his own behavior, motives, and feelings. He'd taken a psychology class during his junior year, talked with me about diagnoses, syndromes, mental health, and disorders. And at the same time, his thinking became more fluid and rational; he seemed suddenly socially *smarter*. Smarter about himself and smarter about others.

In Ventura, we toured the movie studio–cum–film school and we walked on the Southern California beach at sunset. We were impressed with the school's equipment, the possibilities for filmmaking jobs after graduation. I loved the beach towns; I could see visiting a kid in college there. On the ride home, we talked about the downside, though: no dorms, no true college experience, the expense! But my imagination didn't take me farther than that. My mother protection denial device was still activated. It was all still so abstract, the thought of Matt going to college, going away from us. What I'd often longed for, I now began to dread, like any other parent, I guessed.

The following month, we headed north to a state university where we spoke with the director of special services and to the chair of the theater, dance, and film school, checked out the dorms, and ate in the cafeteria. A week later,

we visited a campus in Monterey. On the drive down, Patty
and I recalled choosing our colleges from brochures instead of
visits. But we knew Matt had to see his choices, had to
physically check out this abstraction called college. For months
after the visits, Matt would not list the schools by priority. He
could not make a decision, did not know how. Patty and I
began talking to each other in front of him, sharing our
impressions, our thoughts about the pros and cons of each
place. We knew he needed time to make sense of it all, to
make this huge decision.

One afternoon near the end of Matt's senior year of high
school, I left the school where I was working and drove the
couple of miles to Matt's private school, where I met up with
Patty. Together we found seats in Matt's English classroom
behind the two teachers who would grade his senior project.
Matt's research project—a paper and PowerPoint presentation
—was a short lesson about Asperger's. His Asperger's, in
particular, and what he now understood about himself, how he
understood his way of learning, and how it made doing school
work so difficult for him.

He'd been talking a lot with us at home about Asperger's
and what had helped him and what had not, but I hadn't seen
his PowerPoint. Dressed in his black umpiring pants and the
orange dress shirt—Giants' orange—that he'd worn to the
winter ball, Matt set up his laptop and, following a nod from
one of his teachers, began explaining the slides. After a brief
overview of Asperger's, he presented his theory about what
had made it so difficult for him to get schoolwork done. They
included environmental factors like hunger and lack of sleep.
And he outlined a tiered set of circumstances—his procras-

tination, motivation, and mood—that, along with pervasive anxiety, had overwhelmed him and shut him down, made it often impossible to manage the load.

As he spoke, I thought of the fifth grade boy whose meeting I'd just left, the boy whose private psychologist swore he was not "Rain Man" but that he had OCD and ADHD. I wondered if that boy would ever stand up in high school and give a report about how he had come to understand himself.

Sitting there in Matt's English class, I wished the public school district's special education gatekeepers could have seen his senior project so they could learn something that would help them teach other kids like Matt. That they'd know that if you've met someone with Asperger's, you've met *one person* with Asperger's.[79] That even though a disability might not be obvious, some students need us to educate them in a different way.

I wish we had known how to help Matt shift more easily between ideas or activities and to consider other people's points of view. And, especially, how to calm himself. Now there are myriad books that show parents and teachers how to alleviate kids' anxiety,[80] avoid tantrums or meltdowns, and teach kids to manage everyday stresses caused by sensory overload and social ignorance.[81] There is now a magazine[82] whose advisory board reads like the All-Star team lineup of autism experts that provides news and research for lay readers—

---

[79] This saying is attributed to Tony Attwood.

[80] Some clinicians successfully utilize a modified version of cognitive behavior therapy with children on the spectrum. Most recommend using concrete materials like charts or diagrams in order to appeal to visual processing preferences of their clients.

[81] See, for example, the Michelle Garcia Winner (et al.) *Superflex* series for children and Elizabeth A. Sautter's guide, *Make Social Learning Stick!*

[82] *Autism Spectrum Quarterly.*

parents and teachers of kids on the spectrum. There are now companies that make seamless socks and underwear, which parents can order for their children online.

We learned so much by trial and error, learning to give him plenty of warning if our plans were changing, keeping his sleeping and eating schedule consistent, and writing out plans, expectations, and rules. We worked with occupational thera-pists and their Brain Gym[83] activities; now the occupational therapists I work with frequently offer kids sensory diets.[84] I've learned from occupational therapists how neurotypical adults use sensory activities to maintain alertness during the day: we drink coffee, chew on crunchy crackers, and take the stairs to the copy machine. To calm ourselves, we take lavender baths, listen to music, watch television. There is a plethora of websites to peruse for help. And now, there are computer apps, so many apps, to help kids with organization and getting tasks done. There are now video games that claim to teach social skills. Their developers, probably more than a few of whom fall somewhere on the autism spectrum themselves, understand the irony of teaching social skills via an electronic device, but they believe the safety of the gadget allows kids to learn through play. Finally, the therapists are catching up; recently I've consulted with several private practitioners about students and have not had to give my "autism is a wide spectrum" speech.

But I also believe that even if Patty and I knew then what we know now, it may have made little difference. We had to find our way, and along the way work with the therapists we needed at each stage. And Matt had to make that cognitive

---

[83] The effectiveness of the curricula is not strongly supported by research.

[84] Sensory activities that allow children to engage in social interactions, self-soothe, and sustain attention.

leap that happened around the time he turned seventeen, when he could begin to think about his behavior, about his thoughts, about who he was. Now, when he disagrees with me about something, he says, "Just try to see my perspective!" And I usually say, "Well, please try to see mine!"

I still get excited about the changes in this fascinating field. The diagnoses du jour change so rapidly; ADHD and autism spectrum disorder, for example, have been in the spotlight recently. As I write this, executive functioning disorder is rearing its head and demanding attention. Children with attention deficit and autism spectrum disorders, as well as a slew of other conditions, can have difficulties with time management, planning ahead, and regulating their emotions because of delays or anomalies in the development of their frontal lobes, the conductor of the symphonies that are our brains.

At an information-rich workshop[85] on a recent Saturday, I was blown away by the cutting-edge interventions for kids with executive functioning difficulties. Once again a professional-turned-mother at a conference, I scribbled notes to share with Matt: Stress is not a sign of failure, so one doesn't need to shut down or give up. Executive functioning is a social skill since it requires coordinating with people. And, the most important idea for my boy who is still struggling with exactly this: Motivation can be thought of as "imagining the emotion of the future," like the pride or relief we will feel when we complete a difficult task, a skill which is so problematic for people on the spectrum.

It was almost tangible, Matt's developmental leap during his junior year of high school. One evening, we all were

---

[85] Sarah Ward, M.S., CCC-SLP.

getting ready to go see the Robert Downey, Jr. *Sherlock Holmes* movie, one of the few movies that all four of us could agree on. Even though he'd been planning on joining us, as the three of us were heading out the door, Matt still didn't have his shoes tied. He sat in the chair by the picture window, one long leg crossed over the other, his shoelaces dangling.

"I don't know if I want to go," he said. It was a school holiday, and he'd been playing a computer game for hours.

"Oh, come on," I said. "We've been planning this all day."

"I don't know."

"It'll be fun. And we'll come right back so you won't miss your precious computer game time." I hated the time both boys spent in front of the computer screen, but that battle had been long given up. I really wanted him to join us for the rare family outing. I tried a few more ploys, appealing to his sense of fairness ("You promised us") and his sense of guilt ("This is a special occasion") but he just became more agitated, and his tone turned to that old familiar one of pre-tantrum. Patty and Spencer headed out the door to avoid the building tornado.

"I don't know if I should go!" he shouted, starting to tie one shoe.

"Okay," I said. "Fine. Don't go." I didn't hide my disappointment behind a cheery tone.

"You're stressing me out!" he said.

"I just said that you can stay home. Don't worry about it."

"But that's stressing me out!"

"Getting what you want?"

"You'll be disappointed if I don't go to the movie. You'll be all, 'It was a really good movie, I wish you'd gone with us.'" He imitated me, mimicking my wounded tone, my accusing tone perfectly.

I was so surprised at his ability to understand my feelings

of disappointment and to articulate the stress it was causing him—instead of throwing his shoe across the room or swiping the books and magazines onto the floor—that I needed a moment to re-form my typical response.

"Okay," I said, changing my tone, trying hard to take advantage of the opportunity to handle this better. "I promise I won't hold it against you."

He finished the shoelace, started on the other.

I continued, "I will be disappointed because I really wanted this to be a family movie. But I understand. You want to stay here. I won't be mad at you."

He stopped tying his shoe. "Really?"

"Really. It's okay."

And it was.

Near the end of his final semester of high school, Matt's GPA hung less than a percentage point from the cutoff for the state university where he'd been conditionally accepted. That percentage point was due to his grade in English—dangling between a C or D—and was dependent on his ability to finish two more writing assignments. At the eleventh hour, Matt called me at work. He was walking from school to the BART station on his way home. He wanted to know what to do about the first essay since it was due the next day and he hadn't started it—despite a half-dozen emails between parents and teacher, a face-to-face meeting among him, us, and two of his teachers to see what he needed to complete in order to pass his classes and graduate. I tried my usual tactics: making lots of practical suggestions, pointing out that he'd had two weeks already, and finally, letting him know that his going to either the university or a city college would be fine with us.

"Just be quiet!" he shouted into his cell phone. "I can't think."

"Okay," I said, wounded but also curious.

"Just don't say anything."

"Okay."

"You just said something."

"What?"

"You just said, 'Okay.' Please don't say anything."

I stayed silent.

"Okay, I need to think. I'm going to keep walking."

And there was a pause like no other I'd experienced on the phone with anyone ever before. I could hear his breathing and the rustling made by his walking. And I stayed quiet. I picked at my nails. I straightened every paper and paperclip and Post-it notepad on my desk. And I stayed quiet, listening to my own breathing, too. There had been times while raising Matt that I had longed for silence, but we had been so completely lit on fire by our emotions that we shouted until our throats burned. None of us had any time to think once the battles had begun. Now Matt was asking for that time. Time to hold onto his own thoughts before I started in with suggestions or orders or opinions. He needed to hear what his own head was telling him.

Forty-five seconds of quiet. I checked the clock. I had no more appointments; I could wait as long as he needed. And I realized that I would. I would not speak until he asked me to.

The rumbling of an earthquake for fifteen seconds feels like an eternity when you just want it to stop. Ninety seconds is a long stretch of dead air over a phone line. Except it wasn't dead; it was the antithesis of death. The time Matt took before he spoke again felt like a conception. It was a new way of behaving for him. He was telling me what he needed instead of showing me, instead of exploding from frustration. There were so many times when he had tried to show me and I hadn't understood. But I did then, and even though it almost killed me for at least the first half a minute, I stayed quiet. After that half minute, though, I was nearly euphoric. This was different. And it was good.

When I look back on all those years of not understanding him, I still wonder: Had I the knowledge I have now, would it have made much difference? Could I have just listened and made it all okay? Unlikely. Yes, he needed me to listen, but because he couldn't articulate what he needed, I would have had to read his mind. Earlier, when we became aware of his sensory defensiveness, we bought him clothes he could tolerate. When we realized he had trouble with unstructured time on weekends and holidays, we wrote out lists and schedules. We found professionals to teach him how to keep a conversation going, to take another person's perspective, to understand what he was feeling.

Back then I didn't know what to do when he raged. I could not talk him off the ledge. But it appeared that now I might be able to. By *not* talking.

I imagine what it would be like to start over with Matt. We'd still make mistakes; that's to be expected for all parenting, not just parenting kids with extra needs. I think about what we now know about Matt's need for sleep, what we learned from speech and language pathologists about perspective-taking and reciprocal conversations and what we know from the research about brain differences. I wish we'd known how to help him better cope with his hypersensitive sensory integration system. I wish we'd learned more about tantrums and how to help Matt regulate his emotions. I understand now that they were not like a typical two-year-old's tantrums, functioning to test limits or to gain autonomy. They were similar in that they were born from frustration and an inability to express the reason for the frustration, but they were caused by a plethora of reasons: sensory, cognitive, and social. We also needed to know, to really understand, that Matt's brain worked differently. That he needed a type of parenting that we didn't know how to provide. We were learning it as we were living it, and we all know that a maelstrom of stress is not the ideal condition for learning.

I know now that my insistence on a behavioral modification model was not ideal. Matt told us this over and over, but I lacked another way. Coupled with another method, like the SCERTS[86] model, or Ross W. Greene's[87] Collaborative Problem Solving, we might have been more successful. Matt said over and over that negative consequences didn't work and only made him more frustrated or angry. I wish we had trusted that he knew, at least partially, what he needed from us.

I wish I'd had more skills in preventing tantrums, helping him with his inflexibility in particular. I wish, and this is probably the most difficult admission, that I had done better at working on my own inflexibility, my own need to be right, my need to be obeyed because that's the way I was raised: to obey one's parents. I wish I could have been a different kind of parent for my son, but I also know I did the best I could and that I don't need to berate myself over my shortcomings.

I was not a perfect mother; I was a fantastic mother and a crappy mother, which I hope averages out to pretty decent, or good enough. I'm a Virgo, firstborn, female, Type A perfec-

---

[86] SCERTS: SC: social communication; ER: emotional regulation; and TS: transactional support (for families). Developed by Barry Prizant, Amy Wetherby, Emily Rubin, and Amy Laurent.

[87] Author of *The Explosive Child* and *Lost at School*.

tionist who's pretty tightly wound. I have an overly strong need to please and a mission to not disappoint others. When I was pregnant, the book *What to Expect When You're Expecting* made me feel guilty for eating bagels. My self-doubts likely contributed to my attempts to maintain control in our family.

We're all so much smarter at the end of our parenting run than during it. As soon as we know just about everything about raising kids, the kids are out of the house. I take some consolation in the hope that I can use my experiences to smooth the way for some of the families I work with. And, most of all, I hope for long, loving relationships with my two boys.

I wish I had not gotten stuck on my original vision of Matt's future, that I could have accepted much earlier that he would take his own path—prestigious college vs. state or city college, marrying and having children vs. living alone—that it would be his life. And it would be fine. Knowing this would have alleviated a lot of my own anxiety, which we now know only served to inflame Matt's.

I wish we had sought out contact with other parents so we didn't feel so alone and incompetent. It wasn't until I started asking a few parents from the co-op preschool we'd attended together to read this manuscript that I learned that many other families were struggling with their own children's problems during elementary and middle and high school. We were all covering our shame because we felt we were the only ones. If only we'd been able to help each other. I loved my escapes to solitary pursuits—yoga and walking in the hills—but other times, the isolation was painful.

I don't know how I'd decide on the medication if I had to do it over. Matt resents us forcing him to take it, and I feel jolts of guilt when I think about it at times. He told me recently that he remembers stopping the medication and "for the first time feeling what I was feeling." But that's precisely why we looked to medicine for help. His feelings were flooding him, and when he didn't understand them, or know how to soothe himself, he ended up nearly destroying the house. Plus he was miserable—a sobbing, unhappy mess. And so were we.

While I sat at my desk at work that day Matt called me about his English assignments, he began to talk. He talked for three minutes. I stayed quiet. Finally, he stopped and was quiet for a few seconds. Then he took a breath. "Why," he asked, "aren't you saying anything?"

Wearing a royal blue cap and gown draped with a white lei— and a black Giants tee shirt underneath—Matt graduated in a senior class of fifteen kids instead of the eight hundred from his original high school class. That day in June, my mother and brother joined Patty, Spencer, and me at the school to witness Matt shaking his filmmaking teacher's hand and receiving his diploma from the school's director. Student speakers told of their experiences in public schools—smart kids failing classes because they were not able to focus long enough or they couldn't process information presented via lecture or they couldn't understand the sophisticated social expectations of their peers. They all felt stupid until they came to this school where teachers finally understood them. Where they were given the space to show their stuff.

The month before, at the school's athletic banquet, a silent slide show had played during the potluck dinner, photos of the kids competing against other small high schools throughout the year. And this time, unlike his absence in the crew photos his freshman year, Matt's photo appeared again and again. But one stuck with me and made me fight grateful tears. My six-foot one-inch son towers over the others on his flag football team, all huddled to hear the play. Matt's wild curly blond hair shines in the late afternoon light, and a swath of ruddy beard lines his jaw. And he is laughing.

That night at the banquet, a bunch of kids who wouldn't have made it on a sports team at their local school were being called to the stage to pick up MVP awards, giddy with pride.

Some of the graduating students thanked their teachers and their parents for sending them to the small school. "At first I was really mad at my parents for forcing me to come here," the girl who took calculus with Matt said, "but once I got here, it felt like home."

If it takes a village to raise a child these days, then it takes a village of specialized members to raise a child on the autism spectrum. We worked with many competent, caring professionals over the years, and were grateful for them all. They were part of our mini-village, they truly cared about Matt, and shared with us in the raising of him. Our helpers tended to come sequentially, though, and we worked generally with only one at a time, in what now seems a rather piecemeal approach. At work, I'm part of a team that comes together first to assess what a kid needs and then to organize a menu of services to provide it.

A *New York Times Magazine* article[88] profiled a young girl who could not feel pain and needed to be taught repeatedly what could cut or burn her and how to avoid those injuries. Similarly, children on the spectrum need to be taught directly and repeatedly the specific skills that make up social thinking

---

[88] November 12, 2012.

and cognitive flexibility. Since their needs encompass several fields of expertise, they often need this teaching from a team of experts.

We know now that most kids on the spectrum need a village of professionals like occupational therapists, speech and language therapists, teachers, psychotherapists, and sometimes MDs. All of these practitioners need to work with the child's parents, who are the captains of the team, to mix metaphors.[89] After almost three decades as a school psychologist, I'm still learning. I have to keep current with newer methods of assessment[90] and with the revisions to those I have been trained to use.[91] It keeps the job fresh and my brain limber. But it's really the kids who keep me curious, captivated, and content with the job. As I did at the beginning of my career, I feel like a detective putting all of the clues together to discover what's going on with each child. And hopefully once we know that, we can get them what they need in order—as Matt put it once —to live, learn, and change.

· · ·

---

[89] A good psychological evaluation for autism spectrum disorder will always include multiple measures. I place the highest value on a thorough developmental history (baby books, photo albums, and videos can help parents remember the early years); school report cards, which can give clues about early social development (red flags include multiple preschools attended and social problems at recess, for example); observing the child in structured and unstructured situations with same-age peers; querying the student's teachers about learning styles and social skills (children on the spectrum often get along better and can be more engaging with adults than peers); interviewing (and chatting with) the student; and using both nonstandardized and standardized measures of cognition, perception, executive functioning, and social thinking
  with the understanding that children can score within normal limits on such tests but not be able to demonstrate skills in the natural environment.

[90] *The Denver Model* and the *Autism Spectrum Rating Scales* for example. Also, Michelle Garcia Winner uses a double interview and other nonstandardized methods of assessing social thinking skills.

[91] *Autism Diagnostic Observation Schedule (ADOS-2)*, for example.

Photos of the public high school graduation—of Matt's former classmates—began showing up on Facebook. The parents of kids we'd known since preschool had posted pictures of their kids in matching gowns and decorated caps marching across the school's stage. We'd always imagined ourselves sitting in that theater on that day, so the photos had a sting to them. But we'd taken a detour off that path, followed Matt as he made his way down a different one. And it was okay.

18

Beginnings

W HEN YOU TAKE YOUR FIRSTBORN TO COLLEGE—AN
event you've anticipated for eighteen years—you know
you will cry when you say good-bye.

When we were fifteen minutes away from his college campus, I
reached behind my front passenger seat and tapped Matt on
the knee to get his attention. He pulled out the ear buds that
had been piping music into his head for three hours, and I
said, "Can we have ten minutes?"

"What for?" he asked, and I told him we knew he'd do great
at college and reminded him about crazy, life-threatening
hazing rituals, and begged him not to get into cars with drunk
drivers. I told him I knew he couldn't wait to get rid of us and
start his new life, and he smiled and nodded. I told him, "You
will get homesick. Not for a while, but you will."

We passed a mall with a Bed Bath & Beyond, and I
interrupted what he was saying to point them out in case he'd
forgotten anything. He scowled and raised his voice, shouting
about being interrupted, and I started to cry way before I
thought I'd cry on this trip. Then I understood what was hap-

pening and told him it was pretty typical that we were having a fight in the car on the way to this momentous occasion. Patty and I would talk with other parents during orientation who'd had squabbles in the car on the way. Matt nodded, glared at me, and plugged his ear buds back in.

When the last parent orientation meeting was over, I texted Matt to meet us at the van. As Patty and I walked back across the huge parking lot, I remembered Matt's first day of kindergarten and how I cried all the way to work, a cord of pain whipping through my body. I had figured this drop-off would be similar. I had no idea it would be so much more agonizing.

There were many, many times that I'd prayed for this day to come, that I'd wanted him the hell out of my face, out of the house. But those times had dimmed, much like memories of childbirth do, and all I felt that day was the doom of impending loss, a new hole ripping through my heart.

As Patty and I prepared to launch Matt, we knew it was time to focus on Spencer, our Mellow Man, the tag-along kid who had suffered during the years of tantrums and family upset, who continued to have to make adjustments for his brother and deal with the inequalities of our parenting.

Moving Matt's boxes and computer and wide-screen TV from the van to his dorm room, I smiled at other parents on their way in and out, but the smile was faked. I wanted to sob and exclaim to them, *Can you believe we're doing this? What's this like for you? How do we drive home now, not knowing what our kids are doing, if they're okay?* But I'm always embarrassing my children, and I have enough social skills—most of the time—to just keep my mouth shut.

Matt and I had met one of the guys in his suite and, when

the boy turned away, we immediately exchanged the look that means *my autism radar just beeped*, and we smiled at each other, trying not to laugh out loud in front of the kid. Matt would tell me later that we'd been right, and actually there were three boys on the spectrum in his suite, making me wonder what was up in the housing department when they grouped first year students that year or whether it had been a random selection process and there just were that many.

Matt and I have compared notes on people we've met over recent years, and we sometimes discuss our particular family's genetic mapping. We may never know if the sperm donor brought us the Asperger's or if it came from my side of the family tree. Like most families, we have quirky members, but no one else has been given the official diagnosis. One of my grandfathers was a scientist, and he loved to map out the most efficient routes for car trips. "This way is approximately an eighth of a mile longer but three minutes quicker," he'd say. Perhaps he simply preferred precision, or perhaps his manner would rate him a spot on the spectrum we now know includes a slew of smart and successful people.

Matt was at the van, and as I reached up, he leaned over to hug me. I grabbed onto my six-foot one-inch firstborn, and my eyes filled. When we pulled apart, Matt smiled at the predicted tears while I whispered, "I love you, big boy." I tried to smile, but my face couldn't do it. I said, "Skype me, damn it," in the way I did, having been the mother of two boys for a long time. A couple at their own van turned to witness our parting. We'd seen a few fathers that day wiping away tears and blowing their noses.

Inside the van, I found a tissue to sop up my tears, now streaming. I rolled down my window and said "I love you" one more time, and Matt smiled and waved and started walking across the long parking lot back to his dorm. Patty waited a minute before pulling away so I could watch him until he was hidden by parked cars, then I put on my seatbelt and folded the tissue into eighths, creasing each fold over and over.

When we pulled out of the lot, I looked back, longing to see him again. It had become terribly important; it was almost superstitious, my desperate need to see him one last time or I feared something horrible would happen. And as the van turned onto the road toward home, I spotted, all the way across the parking lot, the orange Giants tee shirt and the blond head of my firstborn bobbing away from me.

Afterword

When Matt read this manuscript before it went to press, he told me he thought I'd tied the story up too neatly, that I'd given the impression that things are all fine now. "It's only because we don't live together that things are a little better," he said. He reminded me that he still gets extremely frustrated when Patty or I are not explicit when we talk with him. "There's still a lot of tension when we get together," he said. "If we were living in the same house again, I'd be blowing up sometimes."

I, too, get exasperated when we spend more than a couple of hours together, when we struggle to communicate. "I need more context," I tell him, because he sometimes forgets that I don't have access to all the information that he carries around in his head. He assumes I know what he's talking about even when a significant part is missing—an important puzzle piece that prevents me from seeing the whole picture.

His need for exactness makes me more precise in my emails and texts. I don't abbreviate much, I don't assume he'll know what I'm talking about, so I probably give too much prelude, and I edit heavily before I hit send.

He still has trouble when we change plans on him too quickly; he needs enough warning in order to shift to something he wasn't expecting. I still push him too much at times, trying to see whether he can flex a bit more or a bit faster. Sometimes he can, sometimes he cannot. He is now better able to regulate his emotions; he credits his maturity, the behaviorists who once worked with him, and medical marijuana for helping the most.

At first, Patty and I fought hard against the marijuana use, and around the same time I remember being alarmed to learn that some parents of children with severe forms of autism were medicating them with cannabis edibles with the hope of reducing violent behavior. But until you've walked a mile in someone else's shoes...I've come a long way, as they say. I've witnessed the limitations of traditional psychotropic medications as well as their unpleasant side effects. I don't like the reported harmful effects of marijuana use on developing brains, and I'd much prefer a safer option. However, I understand why so many kids with anxiety, ADHD, and autism spectrum disorders, for example, are self-medicating with marijuana. And Matt, with his rigorous research,[92] has convinced me that we should not rule out the potential benefits of cannabis for a number of physical ailments and neurologic disturbances, and I understand his attraction to its anti-anxiety and pro-social properties. I rolled my eyes when he compared his marijuana use to me going out for a drink with friends after work, but I am beginning to get it.

He and I are now talking. At twenty-one, Matt has talked on the phone with me for over an hour a few times. Phoning and texting have always been the best modes for us when discussing difficult subjects; it feels safer with that protective curtain between us filtering the anxiety to which we're both susceptible. Phone calls can still be full of friction, though, and when our voices get raised I often have to demand a break. Then I move to emailing and texting for the slow-down-and-think-about-what-you-want-to-say protection it can provide.

---

[92] He got an A on his speech arguing for legalization of marijuana during his first year at college. I have to admit I was proud.

But each time I hear Matt's familiar vocal crescendo, I feel the old steel doors lock into place. I come from a long line of conflict avoiders, and my preferred method of handling disputes is to take a nap. Like lots of other couples, Patty and I had very few conflicts until we started parenting, and then our smallest differences in style swelled like those smooshed sponge-animal capsules when they're dropped into water. Matt still gets stuck sometimes on the way he would like things to be, and when he winds up I still want to run screaming from the house while pulling out clumps of my hair. Instead, I usually just hang up the phone and pace the house until I can breathe deeply again.

At the time of this writing, Matt has taken a break from college, lives on his own in a city several hours away from us, and works at an almost full-time job. He has strong opinions about the failure of traditional education for people who learn differently or have trouble with motivation, and he does not understand the relevance of sitting in a lecture hall listening to something that doesn't interest them. Matt swears that he learned more from a few months one summer listening to podcasts and public radio than he did in two years of college.

He and I have talked about his childhood, the trials and joys of those years, what we his parents did wrong and what we did right, what he resents, what he appreciates. He is not ashamed of the Asperger's or worried about people knowing about it; however, he does not want people to behave differently around him because of it. He also reminds me that this story spotlights the worst of his behavior during his childhood, but that those scenes are necessary to tell the story. "If you cut out the worst scenes," he said, "you'd just sound like a whining mom." I was floored at this understanding of perspective—potential readers' and mine. Matt would prefer to tell his childhood story from his point of view and on his own timeline, and he reminds me that the story does not show the whole person, his true personality or character or, as I would call it, his extraordinary soul.

Acknowledgments

Thanks first to Patty for trusting me to tell our story. And to our sons, both of whom make me so proud. Deep gratitude to all of the professionals, colleagues, friends, and relatives who helped us through the roughest years. I am grateful beyond words to the readers of the manuscript for their help in making it better: Liz Angoff, Peter August, Rebecca Branstetter, Colleen Morton Bush, Gina Cobin, Michele French, Christin Geall, Patsie Kao, Annie Kassof, Suzanne LaFetra, Karin Larsen, Marjorie McAneny, Kathy Morrisroe, Suzanne Popkin, David Raether, Lisa Romeo, Holly Rose, Heidi Sawicki, Eva Schlesinger, Laura Shumaker, Jennifer Simmons, Nan Steinley, Sonia Thacher, and Wilma Wyss. To my publishing team: Luan Stauss of Laurel Books, Aleta George, Stacey Aaronson, the 1106 Design team, Barbara Weaver, Carrie Rodrigues, and Marta Tanrikulu, thank you.

About the Author

Anne K. Ross is the pen name for an award-winning writer and school psychologist with three decades of experience working in public schools in Northern California. She holds a master's degree in educational psychology, a Ph.D. in clinical psychology, and an MFA in creative writing. She is a past winner of an American Psychological Association dissertation research award, and she has published in professional and literary journals. Her creative writing has been nominated for a Pushcart Prize and a Lambda Literary Award. She is the mother of two young adult sons.

Find her at BeyondRainMan.com or @annerossrainman

CPSIA information can be obtained
at www.ICGtesting.com
Printed in the USA
FSOW01n2340230116
16092FS